SAXONS VS. VIKINGS

SAXONS VS. VIKINGS
Alfred the Great and the Birth of England

Ed West

Part One of West's Histories

First published in 2017 by Skyhorse Publishing

Revised and expanded edition published in 2023 by
Sphinx Books
London

Copyright © 2023 by Ed West

The right of Ed West to be identified as the author of this work has been asserted in accordance with §§ 77 and 78 of the Copyright Design and Patents Act 1988.

All rights reserved. No part of this publication may be reproduced, stored in a retrieval system, or transmitted, in any form or by any means, electronic, mechanical, photocopying, recording, or otherwise, without the prior written permission of the publisher.

British Library Cataloguing in Publication Data

A C.I.P. for this book is available from the British Library

ISBN-13: 978-1-91-595-205-9

Typeset by Medlar Publishing Solutions Pvt Ltd, India

www.aeonbooks.co.uk/sphinx

Cover art by Margaux Carpio

CONTENTS

INTRODUCTION												vii

CHAPTER 1
Rome answers the appeals of the Britons: no, says Rome			1

CHAPTER 2
When the Angles met the Saxons									11

CHAPTER 3
The world of Beowulf: Northumbrian golden age					25

CHAPTER 4
Return of the kings: from Oswald to Offa						37

CHAPTER 5
What the Vikings did for us										47

CHAPTER 6
Wessex: the last kingdom										63

CHAPTER 7
The life of Alfred   77

CHAPTER 8
The first king of England   91

CHAPTER 9
Alfred's legacy   101

BIBLIOGRAPHY   109

ENDNOTES   111

INDEX   115

INTRODUCTION

The Vikings first set foot in England in the year 789, near Portland in what was then the kingdom of Wessex. As they came ashore on the south coast, a local official called Beaduheard walked up to their leader and explained that under government regulations they had to pay docking duties. The chief Viking put an axe through his head. Or as the *Anglo-Saxon Chronicle* reported, "the reeve rode thither and tried to compel them to go to the royal manor, for he did not know what they were; and then they slew him".[1] Community relations were off to a tricky start.

It was the first of many such cultural misunderstandings: four years later the Vikings attacked the holy island of Lindisfarne in the northern kingdom of Northumbria, killing a number of monks and taking the others off to a presumably grim life of slavery. The Lindisfarne massacre took place on June 8, 793, the feast day of Medard, patron saint of toothaches and the weather, and followed some bad omens of comets, whirlwinds, and fiery dragons seen in the sky. It was said in Europe that bad weather on St Medard's Day would result in weeks of the same, so it was considered a terrible portent for the heathens to attack that day, although in fairness there was probably never a good day for a Viking raid; worse still, earlier that year people in York had seen blood dripping from the roof of the city's St Peter's church.

Although the Vikings soon disappeared from the coast of England and remained quiet for several decades, the raiders returned in the 830s and the number of attacks began to increase alarmingly. In 850 they overwintered for the first time, and in 865 launched a full-scale invasion, a takeover so effective that by the year 871 three of the four Anglo-Saxon kingdoms had been conquered. The last kingdom, Wessex, now faced collapse as large Danish armies overwhelmed the smaller and less organised groups of native forces. It was at this point that fate pushed forward a man who would shape an entire nation's history.

England may have never come to exist were it not for this one man, and it is with good reason that Alfred is the only English king to be known as "the Great".[2] He fought off the Danes; he helped found a common law for everyone; he built towns for the first time since the Romans left; he introduced a navy (well, sort of); and he also he encouraged education in a country just emerging from centuries of illiteracy. Learning to read in adulthood, King Alfred personally translated Latin texts into English and was the only king to write anything before Henry VIII, as well as the only European ruler between the second and thirteenth centuries to write on the philosophy of kingship.[3] Perhaps most of all, though, it was Alfred, along with his son, daughter and grandson, who would join together the kingdoms of the Anglo-Saxons to create one united England.

What's more surprising is that Alfred, the fifth and youngest son of King Ethelwulf, was a sickly and neurotic individual who comes across almost as a Woody Allen figure thrown into the horror of early medieval battle, forced to spend his time fleeing from marauding bands of Viking maniacs when he would much rather have been a scholar stuck in a monastery reading the Bible and making beer. As he wrote much later in his translation of the Roman book *On the Consolation of Philosophy*, "the greatness of this earthly power never will please me, nor did I altogether very much yearn after this earthly authority".

After coming to the throne at the height of the Viking invasion, Alfred would spend the next seven years on the run, eventually living out in a bog, and on several occasions he was almost captured—and considering that two of the other English kings in the past decade had been tortured to death, it was not an attractive prospect. And as if things weren't terrible enough, he also had an extremely painful chronic stomach condition throughout his adult life. Yet by the time he died, in 899, Wessex was safe, half of the neighbouring kingdom of Mercia had been taken back from the Vikings, the derelict Roman city of London rebuilt, and Alfred's family were on the way to conquering all of England. His grandson Athelstan would finish his mission twenty-eight years later, uniting the country under borders that remain roughly the same today. By the end of the millennium "Englalond" was perhaps the most sophisticated state in western Europe, with the currency it still has today, the beginnings of a jury system, and a flourishing, highly literate Church.

It was a far cry from its origins a few centuries earlier, during a period usually called the Dark Ages, when their ancestors arrived in the crumbling last days of Roman rule.

CHAPTER 1

Rome answers the appeals of the Britons: no, says Rome

"The groans of the Britons ... The barbarians drive us to the sea, the sea drives us to the barbarians; between these two means of death, we are either killed or drowned." So wrote the leaders of the province of Britannia in their final appeal to the Romans around the middle of the fifth century.

This message was recorded by Gildas, a depressive sixth-century monk who chronicled the collapse of the country in his rather downbeat book (as hinted at by its title), *The Ruin and Conquest of Britain*. The barbarians he referred to were raiders from across the North Sea, whom Gildas would have called *Saesneg* or *Garman* (Germans) but have become known to us as Anglo-Saxons. The first chapter in the history of England begins with these invaders who, three and a half centuries later, faced the same fate themselves at the hands of a new wave of scary barbarians.

The Portlane reeve of 789 and his new Viking friends, who were probably from Hordaland or Hardangerfjord in Norway, might have been able to understand each other quite well, since the Anglo-Saxons had themselves once been pagan invaders from a similar part of the world, and the native Britons had then viewed their arrival with a similar lack of enthusiasm.

The story behind both the Saxon and Viking invasions is told in *The Anglo-Saxon Chronicle*, one of two works commissioned by King Alfred in the ninth century, the other being a biography written by a Welsh monk called Asser. Both books give Alfred rather a good press, but even taking aside any bias, we know that when he came to power Anglo-Saxon England was close to complete Viking conquest, and when he died Alfred had established a dynasty whose descendants still rule England today. In creating laws and by bringing the country much more firmly under the influence of the Latin cultural world, he also set the ground for the English political and legal system.

Asser was a Welsh monk hired by Alfred during a relatively peaceful period of his rule, which was otherwise mainly characterised by Viking attacks. Asser's biography begins in the biblical style by explaining the king's descent: Alfred was the son of King Ethelwulf of Wessex, who was son of King Egbert, and so on, going back to the earliest rulers of the kingdom, a line which starts with the semi-mythical Cerdic in the sixth century. Cerdic, although his existence is somewhat doubted, was said to be the founder of the kingdom of the West Saxons, sailing over from Germany and arriving in Hampshire in 495. Through Cerdic, Asser traced Alfred's line back to Woden and Geat and various other mythical Germanic figures on the continent, before the family tree inexplicably joins up to the biblical line of Seth and Noah and all the way back to Adam.

The Angles and Saxons who conquered most of what was then the Roman province of Britannia were illiterate, and so their earliest history was recorded by their enemies and victims, the Britons, who unsurprisingly did not give them a very good press. Gildas described the arrival of the Saxons as being like "a pack of cubs" followed by "a larger troop of satellite dogs". The words of help he recalled about the groans of the Britons were perhaps sent in the year 449 to Agitius, consul of Rome, in an appeal for help against the barbarian invaders. The Romans answered their prayers. Unfortunately, the answer was "No," or more precisely "Look after your own affairs."[4]

Writing in the following century, and from the relative safety of Armorica in Gaul, where many Britons had fled, Gildas penned a book cursing not just the Saxons but the various rulers who had brought disaster on Britain. Among these are Constantine, "the tyrannical whelp of the unclean lioness of Damnonia", "thou bear" Cuneglasse, whoever he was, and another, Maglocune, whom he calls the "dragon of the island". Gildas wrote how "The first wave landed on the eastern side of the island ... and there they fixed their terrible claws, as if to defend the country, but in fact to attack it. Their German motherland, seeing them successfully installed, dispatched a wonderful collection of hangers-on and dogs, who, arriving by the boatload, joined up with their misbegotten comrades." He also quoted liberally from the *Book of Revelations*, the biblical book of choice for all lunatics down the ages,[5] and his prose sometimes gets a little heated. Gildas was a sort of proto-doom-mongering newspaper columnist predicting that everything was going to the dogs; and of course, he was completely right—Britain was doomed.

It was hardly the best of times for anyone. The map of Europe at the end of the fourth century resembles a chaotic weather chart, full of arrows that record the movements of various tribes making their way across the continent in enormous war bands of up to 80,000 people. Some of them were escaping various climate-related disasters in a period of volatile weather; some were running away from other groups of barbarians.

The Vandals came from what is now Poland and travelled to Germany, then France and down to Spain, before crossing over to Tunisia and then to Sicily, eventually sacking Rome in 455; their name survives in Andalucía (and for those who mindlessly smash things up, although by most accounts they weren't the worst).[6] The Visigoths started out in Romania and invaded Greece before landing in southern Italy and going up and down the entire length of the country and then settling in central Spain, where they ruled for several centuries, abandoning paganism and becoming enthusiastically intolerant Christians.

And while the Black Sea was being raided by Goths and Heruls from Scandinavia as far back as the third century, the northern shore of the empire in what is now Belgium was attacked by a "confederation of many tribes" calling themselves the Franks. The Romans eventually regained control on both sides of the English Channel and began to build what are usually called the "Saxon shore-forts", most likely by employing barbarians from Saxony to protect the region; eventually large numbers of Saxons were used to defend Britain from other alarming long-haired Germans.

But of all the barbarians, the Huns were the most adventurous, and terrifying, originating in central Asia and travelling across the vast Eurasian steppes before reaching Transylvania, where they split up, one group arriving somewhere near Paris and the other invading Italy. Even the sort of grunting, hairy-faced Goths and Vandals who gave Romans sleepless nights were themselves terrified of the Huns, who had introduced the stirrups from central Asia and so vastly increased the area horsemen could cross. This only encouraged further Germanic expansion into Roman territory, as generally the Huns didn't make very good neighbours.

Why was Rome collapsing? There were a number of reasons, but the decline was so slow and the argument so well-trodden over that you could write a sixteen-volume book about it. The empire had problems with inflation, it had problems with powerful generals starting civil wars, it had a massive problem with birth rates, and with the barbarian tribes on its doorstep, who had become too numerous to deal with. Perhaps the biggest problem of all was disease, with the empire hit by successive waves of horrific plagues from the third century onwards, reducing its ability to support a state system with taxes, or defend the frontier. Climate change was also a factor, as the mild years of the "Roman climatic optimum" (from 250 BC to AD 400) gave way to the freakish cold of late antiquity.

In the year 286 the eastern and western halves of the empire had been divided between different rules and, while united once again, that division would become permanent in the fourth century, with the wealthier half now ruled from Constantinople. The western empire began to run out of soldiers, unable to pay a declining population depleted by disease. At this time, the army in Britain shrinks in size, and begins to retreat from outlying areas. There are increasing numbers of attacks, from the Picts to the north, from the Irish and from Germanic sea raiders. The later Roman period is also characterised by a large uptick in later-discovered hoards, which are reliable measures of pessimism and disorder, with rates reaching ten a year by AD 400 (compared to about three a year over the entire Roman period). In 402 come the last Roman coins made in Britain.

Bit by bit the more distant parts of the western empire began to be settled by Germans, with imperial armies no longer having the strength to oppose them. The Britons now found that top of the "what the Romans did for us" list was "security". To the north the Picts, related to the Britons though in cultural terms not close enough to be invited over for Christmas, had been kept out for four centuries by the Roman army stationed on Hadrian's Wall (if that's why they built the wall. Some historians doubt its purpose although it seems sort of obvious what a wall is for). But with the Roman army gone, they began raiding and pillaging from their Caledonian homeland into what had been the province of Britannia. The Britons asked the imperial army to help them, but Emperor Honorius had his own problems, as the Visigoths had just sacked Rome and kidnapped his aunt.

And while Romans cried laments about the ruin of their crops and the slaughter of their families, other people had to deal with climate change as well. At the very north of Germany was the region of Angeln, the "thin peninsula" or "narrow water", low lying and prone to floods.[7] To the south of them lived the Saxons, named after the *scramaseax*, a type of battle knife they were fond of using; and to the north the Jutes. All three tribes (we can guess) faced population pressure at home that made crossing the freezing North Sea to fight Caledonians seem like an attractive prospect. And luckily the collapse of Western civilization brought with it certain job opportunities in what we'd now call the security industry.

Unable to defend themselves from the maniacs on their border, the British leaders decided that the best way to get rid of scary barbarians was to hire other scary barbarians to fight them. A foolproof plan, and one that made sense at the time; after all, the Romans had been using Saxons as hired muscle for centuries and they hadn't tried to violently take over any provinces so far.

There had been a large German community in Norfolk as far as back as AD 320, while Germans of various kinds had been fighting in the Roman army in Britain for far longer, although not with entirely successful results. One of the first mention of Germans on the island dates from AD 83, when some conscripts murdered their commanding officer and other regular soldiers, stole three ships and tried to sail home around Scotland. They were shipwrecked along the way and reduced to eating each other, and when the survivors got home to the Rhineland they were kidnapped by their own people and sold as slaves—to the Romans. How they must have laughed at the irony.

To make matters more confusing, at some point the Britons also rose up against the Romans. Sixth-century Greek historian Zosimus said the Britons "armed themselves, and ran many risks to ensure their own safety, and freed their cities from attacking barbarians … expelling the Roman magistrates and establishing the government they wanted". But the exact details and nuances of this conflict will probably remain a mystery, and all we know is that, once the Romans left, the Britons also descended into fighting among themselves; a series of king-warlords now emerge, some of whose names have survived in legend, among them Old King Cole. Cole, or Coel Hen, may have been a Roman general-turned-usurper (there were plenty of these around) or a native Briton ruling the area known as Hen Ogledd, "old north", that is, northern England and southern Scotland. How a barely historical king living in the fifth century ended up as a popular nursery rhyme in the early eighteenth century is a bit of a mystery, but it was certainly around in Welsh by around 1200. An alternative, more boring explanation is that he was completely made up.

About a century later a far more influential figure called Wyrtgeorn or Vortigen emerged, although "Vortigen" most likely just means "king"; his full title, according to Gildas, was "Vortigen of the repulsive mouth". (Gildas wasn't a fan.)

Vortigen's handling of these admittedly challenging times seems to have fallen short of ideal; either in AD 430 or 449 he hired three boatloads of poor, hungry and violent Jutes, led by two brothers called Horsa and Hengest, "the Horse and the Stallion", to fight the Picts. The mercenaries arrived in the former Roman province of Cantium and brought with them some of their womenfolk, including Hengest's daughter Rowena, said to be a great beauty (or at least by the standards of the Dark Ages, which presumably weren't very high). According to legend Vortigen fell in love with the girl and offered the Jutes the Isle of Thanet (then with the far more Welsh sounding name Ynys Ruym) if he could win her heart.

The tough guys did their job, Vortigen got his girl, and the Jutes were given the small island. However, it should be noted for the sake of pedants that this story is probably entirely fictitious, in fact almost certainly so. One reason for historical scepticism is that stories featuring brothers with alliterative names are quite a common motif, Romulus and Remus being the most famous example. On the other hand, the Anglo-Saxons did go in for this naming style, and all four of Alfred's brothers had names beginning "Ethel". Similarly, invaders arriving in three ships is also a common theme in stories, which invites historians to be sceptical, although Christopher Columbus did arrive in the Americas with three ships, so who knows.

The next time, the Jutes returned with twenty boats, and soon after that with sixty. At this point some of the more pessimistic natives must have wondered if they weren't a bit overstaffed on the mercenary front, and whether in fact this might not be entirely welcome. Vortigen told the Germans they were no longer needed and to go elsewhere, refusing to pay them anymore; the Jutes now rebelled and overran the whole of

Cantium, or Kent as they called it, and to make things worse the Picts joined up with the same people who had been paid to attack them.

Gildas reflects that Hengest and Horsa now won Kent "by mendacious guile".

According to legend, the Jutes and Britons agreed to meet for peace talks, with 300 unarmed men on each side, but before any sort of road map for peace could be laid out Hengest and his men took out their concealed daggers and massacred all but one of the Britons.

The one surviving Briton was, conveniently, Vortigen, so presumably this was how the hapless leader explained the story, which became known as the Treachery of the Long Knives, when he later turned up in Wales; since the Jutes were illiterate and therefore incapable of telling their side of the story, we'll never know.

The Saxons, who had been arriving further up the North Sea coast, took the land on the other side of the Thames Estuary, now called "the Kingdom of the east Saxons", or Essex. Further north still the Angles arrived in areas that would become known as East Anglia, Mercia, and Northumbria. How different these tribes were to start with is hard to say. The Jutes are slightly obscure and the discovery of grave goods in Kent suggests that they were quite different to the Saxons in these fashions, but these were also heavily influenced by the Franks, who also probably turned up at this point. Indeed, as well as the Angles and Saxons there were also probably Frisians and Swedes among the invaders but, to the Britons at least, they must have seemed all the same.

Even the most liberal cultural relativist of the fifth century, if there was such a thing, must have seen the new state of affairs as a backwards step. The Romano-British lived in cities, could read and write, visited public baths, enjoyed the theatre, spoke Latin and drank imported wine. The Britons were civilised, and tried to ignore the invaders like one would ignore a maniac causing a scene on public transport—by giving him a pound in the hope he'll go away.

Gildas, who really didn't appreciate the exciting diversity that the Anglo-Saxons had introduced to his country, calling them "bloodthirsty, proud, parricidal, warlike and adulterous enemies of God", described how the Britons gave the *Garmans* food at first "to shut the dog's mouth" (he was not very keen on dogs either), but each concession was met with fresh demands for land. Of course, no extortionist in history has ever simply left his victim alone so long as they paid out, and the Anglo-Saxons were no different.

The Saxons were not urban sophisticates; they had the front of their heads shaved and hair grown long at the back in order to make their faces look larger and scarier,[8] they probably practised human sacrifice, and possibly drank from the skulls of their enemies. Sidonius Apollinaris, a Roman chronicler of the fifth century, wrote that "the Saxon surpasses all others in brutality",[9] and presumably there was a lot of competition at the time. According to the Roman historian Tacitus the Saxons used to crucify or drown one in ten prisoners.

The invaders only bothered to occupy three Roman cities—Lincoln, Bath, and Cirencester, although they also built a new settlement a mile west of Roman Londinium called Lundenwic. The vast majority settled in small villages, and so following the Saxon conquest most of the Roman cities were deserted, which romantic Victorian historians liked to put down to their ancestors' earthy, honest manliness but was more likely because they didn't know how to operate things like plumbing. The Anglo-Saxons would later write of these ruined Roman cities with a sense of awe and spookiness, and a very bleak, much later Anglo-Saxon poem talks of "the city-buildings crumble; the works of the giants [*enta geweorc*]—decay". These passed away *hund-cnect*—a hundred generations ago. Only giants could have built such things, many thought.

In his usual cheery fashion, Gildas said that "the cities of our country are still not inhabited as they were; even today they are squalid deserted ruins". (Gildas could be quite depressing sometimes.)

Unlike the Romans, the Saxons weren't great road builders, and it wouldn't be until the eighteenth century that improvements were made on many English highways. Their method of architecture—building one-storey homes out of pig dung—rather contrasts with the glories that were Rome. Out also went the rich variety of food that came with being part of a large empire, such as whole roasted boar consumed with figs or drinking Italian wine inside a heated dining room while boys in togas read from Homer; in came porridge, which is what the Anglo-Saxon diet consisted almost entirely of at the time, eaten inside dung-houses.

It's always said of the British that they're slow to rouse, but that eventually they'll face the enemy and beat them. Unfortunately, the Ancient Britons didn't have the Americans on their side or, to use that common historical comparison, Rome. And so as the simple employer/tradesman relationship deteriorated into outright hostility, the Britons were overwhelmed by people Gildas described as "hated by God and men alike".

Again, they appealed to Rome. The Romans didn't even bother replying this time; the old empire was but a shell of its former glory, in retreat on all sides. There was only the haunting radio silence of the disaster movie where the people out in the cabin realise they're all alone. The Romans had by now lost control of Gaul, and Hispania too, and even what was left of the western empire in Italy would soon crumble as yet another epidemic hit them. Western Europe's population fell by as much as two thirds. The period once commonly known as the Dark Ages had begun.

Faced with conquest, the Latin-speaking British elite headed for higher ground, or across the sea to Armorica, which became known as Brittany, or "Lesser Britain" (which is why Britain is "Great Britain"). Today the Breton language, descended from the Brittonic used by the ancient Britons, is still spoken in shrinking numbers in this part of France, which also has a much more "British" feel (i.e., viewed by the rest of the country as being inhabited by alcoholics).

It must have seemed like the end of civilisation for many—but still, at least they got rid of the Picts.

A much later epic poem, called *Armes Prydein Fawr* (*The Prophecy of Britain*), reflects the bitter resentment felt by the Britons as they were driven west. It predicts the day when the Saxon leaders and their lands will burn, while also cursing that old punchbag, Vortigen. Now, it laments, the "slaves from Thanet are our rulers".

The Britons referred to the invaders as the *Saesneg*, as the English are today called by their neighbours to the west (in Scottish Gaelic it is *Sassenach* and in Cornish *Sowsnek*). They in turn described the natives as *Welsh*, which had a variety of meanings but none of them particularly positive, whether "slave", "foreigner", or "dark stranger" (likewise the French-speaking Belgians are called Walloons, and Wallachia in Romania has the same etymology, while Cornwall, Walsall, and Walthamstow in London probably all come from *Wal*). The Welsh, or Cymraeg—the people—also referred to the neighbouring country as "Lloegyr", literally "the lost lands". As for the Germans themselves, they would eventually call their new home *Angelcyn*, or as it was known by the turn of the millennium, *Englalond*.

CHAPTER 2

When the Angles met the Saxons

Many of the characters involved in the Anglo-Saxon invasion are basically mythical, but supposedly the Saxon warlord Elle arrived in what became Sussex around AD 470, followed by Cerdic in Wessex thirty years later, both of whom pushed the Britons out. According to the *Anglo-Saxon Chronicle*, and obviously written much later, Elle defeated the native tribe, Hesta's Folk, whose name survived in Hastings, while another Saxon leader called Port arrived in 501 and with "his two sons Bieda and Mægla came to Britain with two ships to the place which is called Portsmouth and slew a young British man, a very noble man,"[10] but this may be a very convoluted explanation for how the city got its name—rather than just the obvious "mouth of a port".

This situation was mirrored all over western Europe. Elsewhere the Saxons also moved into central Germany, in what is now Saxony, while the Frisians occupied a region on the modern-day Dutch/German border. The Franks overran the north of Roman Gaul, where they adopted the local Latin dialect that would become French. The Vandals in Spain and the Lombards in Italy also eventually became Romanised, perhaps because those provinces had stronger Roman institutions, but in contrast the Anglo-Saxons maintained their Germanic character. Only thirty words in Old English come from Brittonic, mostly topographic names relating to rivers, although many of these are in fact pre-Celtic, deriving from the languages spoken here when the Celts arrived between 700–500 BC.[11]

It's possible that, because the Britons in the southern lowlands had spoken Latin, while Brittonic was spoken in the north, neither language was therefore strong enough to resist the spread and dominance of Old English. But it's also likely that, compared to barbarians in Gaul or Italy, the invaders of Britain came in much larger numbers.

Academics have long argued about how many Anglo-Saxons actually arrived, and whether they drove most of the natives out or a small number intermarried with the locals. Some think the Anglo-Saxons were small in number, perhaps as few as one in twenty of the overall population, while other studies suggest that they were perhaps around a third or more, and far higher in the east of England.[12]

One genetic study showed that Englishmen even from the west of the country were more closely related to the Norwegians than the Welsh less than 100 miles away, and there hasn't been a Viking raiding party in over a millennium. However, to make matters more confusing, there is also the theory that the Angles and Saxons might have always lived in Britain, at least before the Romans, and that during the imperial period the east of the country was already German-speaking (maybe Boudicca had blonde hair). DNA research certainly shows that people have been crossing the North Sea for thousands of years, so it's not impossible.

Certainly, the Angles and Saxons were conscious that their ancestors had crossed the sea from Germany, the earliest recorded histories dating the story of their first arrival in Britain to the 400s. But we also know that Anglo-Saxon laws, such as those of Ine of Wesse, gave a different blood price between *englisc* and *wilisc*, Anglo-Saxon lives usually being worth twice those of Britons, so the latter were obviously incentivised to abandon their older identity.

But how modern historians have viewed the origins of the Anglo-Saxons have often been determined by the politics of their time. The rediscovery of Tacitus's writings in the sixteenth century began a fashion for all things German that was also influenced by the division of western Christianity into a mostly Latin Catholic south and Germanic north. As English national identity became far more identified by its opposition to that world of priests and garlic, so there grew a stronger sense that the English had come from Germany. The great Victorian historian William Stubbs summed this up when he wrote that "The English are not aboriginal, that is, they are not identical with the race that occupied their home at the dawn of history. They are people of German descent in the main constituents of blood, character and language ... in the possession of the elements of primitive German civilization and the common germs of German institutions."

Anglo-Saxonism became an important part of the national political myth, with Magna Carta seen as an extension of ancient Saxon freedoms that dated back to the continent. The great eighteenth-century political philosopher Baron de Montesquieu even believed the English political system came from the forests of Germany.

Yet just as pan-Germanism rose with English national confidence, it had begun to fade following the Franco-Prussian war in 1870, before being totally killed off by the Third Reich. After the Second World War the Victorian idea that the English were largely descended from manly, freedom-loving Saxon settlers gave way to a view that it was merely elite replacement. There was also a new consensus in archaeology that changing patterns found in graves did not reflect population replacement, but merely an exchange of cultural ideas—"pots, not people", as the phrase went. That this quite optimistic view of human nature, in which iron age tribes peacefully traded broaches with each other, became popular immediately following the years 1914–45 is a slight paradox.

By the end of the twentieth century the general consensus was that most English DNA derived not from the Saxons, nor the Celts, but from the various groups who had lived in Britain before the arrival of the Indo-European speakers. Tests linking modern Britons to the ancient skeleton known as Cheddar Man, who died around 9,000 BC, seemed to confirm this.

Yet more recent genetic research has shown a far less happy picture, showing that Cheddar Man's Ice Age people were mostly entirely wiped out by Neolithic farmers from the Mediterranean 6,000 years ago. They were then largely replaced by the Bell Beaker people, who in turn were decimated by the arrival of the Celts from around 700 BC. Similarly, the arrival of the Angles and Saxons would not have been good news, and the latest finding in genetics suggests that the Britons were driven out of the eastern part of the country. On top of this, evidence from female graves suggests that Saxon women also came in quite large numbers.

It would be foolish to declare any debate settled, but the current thinking is that most likely there was a significant migration in the fifth century, and modern English DNA is between a quarter and a half Anglo-Saxon in origin, while in many areas of eastern England the natives were completely driven out.[13] Gildas was basically correct.

Yet many natives would have stayed behind after the Saxon conquest until their descendants eventually adopted the language and culture of the newcomers; a seventh-century law of King Ine of Wessex describes how the Britons are permitted to live in peace in their villages, so long as they keep themselves to themselves, and at least one archaeological find has turned up by a river, a Saxon settlement coexisting with a British one on the other side. There were still British speakers in East Anglia as late as 700, while Britons still had their own district in Exeter until the tenth century, in an area known as Britayne—Little Britain—until much later.

British resistance to the invasion was recalled in epic poems which chart romantic and dashing but highly unsuccessful military adventures. Aneirin, living in what is now Cumbria, wrote the poem *Y Gododdin* in the seventh century recording the British-Saxon wars. In particular it remembers the dead of a British tribe called the Gododdin who attacked the Angles in what is now North Yorkshire around AD 600; the Britons were led by the hapless Mynyddog Mwynfawr, who managed to get every one of his soldiers killed in this not very successful enterprise.

The wars lasted about a century. Around the year 700 a British monk by the name of Nennius first wrote about the exploits of a leader who roused the Britons from defeat and won twelve battles, only to end in glorious failure with inevitable defeat, and death, some time between 515 and 537, at the Battle of Camlann. It grew to become the most famous legend in the world, the story of a man who, despite his exploits being recorded only hundreds of years later and by some of the biggest liars in history, still inspires hopeful treasure hunters to traipse around the West Country looking for his castle. His name, of course, was Arthur, and legend has it that the king of the Britons did not die and is only sleeping, ready to reawaken at the country's hour of need. It's an interesting tale, but is there any truth in the legend of Arthur?

No.

Of all the stories about Arthur—the sword in the stone, the round table, Camelot, the lady of the lake, and Merlin—perhaps the only bit of truth is that someone called Arthur, or more likely Artorius or Ambrosius Aurelianus,[14] had one or two battles with the Saxons, and even this is probably untrue. Most of the legend comes from Geoffrey of Monmouth, an imaginative historian living in the twelfth century. Geoffrey wasn't too interested in tedious historical procedures like using primary sources or written evidence, and preferred to just take a good story and throw in a few busty maidens, mad wizards, and fairies to liven things up. He also confidently stated that the Welsh arrived in Britain from the ancient city of Troy (in modern Turkey) after its destruction by the Greeks, and that Britain was previously inhabited by a race of giants, so we can't be entirely sure he was accurate about everything.

Backing up his story, Geoffrey said he had learned all about Arthur from "a certain very ancient book" he found in Oxford, without ever revealing it. But he told great stories, and these were tremendously popular all over Europe, much to the frustration even of other medieval chroniclers. Later the Arthur story was cynically embellished by English monarchs, including Richard the Lionheart, who just before setting off on a very costly crusade miraculously discovered the bodies of Arthur and his wife Guinevere at Glastonbury Abbey, as well as Arthur's sword. His nephew, another Richard, then spent a vast fortune on building a castle in Cornwall because it was associated with the legendary king.

This was a period of very scarce knowledge, so any speculation about Arthur will always be unprovable. For example, the *Annals of Wales*, the only record of that country at the time, gives as its only news for the whole year 447: "day dark as night", which doesn't give us much to work on.[15] *The Annals*, which may date to the tenth century but probably later, mention twelve of Arthur's battles in total, all of which have a religious air: "The eighth battle was in Fort Guinnion in which Arthur carried the image of St Mary, forever virgin, on his shoulders and that day the pagans were turned to flight and a great slaughter was made on them through the virtue of our Lord Jesus Christ and through the virtue of his mother St Mary the Virgin." The twelfth battle was at Badon Hill, where according to Nennius he allegedly killed 960 of the enemy single-handedly, a spectacular achievement when one considers that he was also carrying a life-size replica of the "cross of our lord Jesus Christ" throughout the engagement in what can only be described as an unorthodox strategy. The poem also says that no one else killed anyone in the entire battle, it was all Arthur; the Saxons just came at him, one by one, like villains in Jackie Chan films. However, Badon Hill, laments Gildas, was "pretty much the last defeat of the villains".

The legend survived in the more remote, mountainous regions of Britain where the old language was still spoken, and in 1113 some French visitors to Cornwall were told about King Arthur, laughed at the ridiculousness of the story, and were pelted with vegetables. By the thirteenth century it had developed so many convoluted subplots that the biblical character Joseph of Arimathea features as a character, having travelled all the way to Britain, something which would have been rather out of the way for a first-century Judean.

However, even though Arthur is a later creation, there clearly were warlords living in strongholds in the west and north, resisting the encroaching Germans in the post-apocalyptic hellscape. Ancient fortresses, such as Cadbury Hill in Somerset, once again became holdouts for people who lived in material conditions which had slipped back by half a millennium. These would have been the closest thing to a real-life "Camelot", a word only made up by a French poet in the twelfth century.

Yet something resembling civilisation perhaps continued. At Tintagel in Cornwall, recently archaeologists discovered the remains of amphorae that had once contained olive oil or wine, as well as fragments of high-quality tableware, imported from the eastern Mediterranean in the late fifth and early sixth centuries, by which point the western Empire had long fallen. Inevitably, this was reported as evidence of a real-life Camelot.

Today the location of a real "Camelot" has been claimed by various regions and their tourist boards; although Cornwall or Cadbury Hill in Somerset have been cited as possible candidates, there are dozens all over Wales and the North-West, and the Scottish borders are also a possibility. Wherever it is, it certainly wouldn't have looked like the magnificent medieval castle of Arthurian legend, which is based on the period, the fifteenth century, when the story was at its most popular. The real Camelot was probably no more than a couple of horse-drawn caravans and a ditch for urinating in, and had she existed Guinevere would have more likely sported the look of the toothless Dark Ages hag dressed in old rags, rather than being a beautiful medieval princess with a cone-shaped hat and perfectly shampooed Rapunzel hair.

Although Arthur was largely made up by chroniclers, the Saxon kings identified as his enemies, Cerdic and his son Cynric, are at least semi-historical, the *Anglo-Saxon Chronicle* recording their arrival either in 495 or 514. Indeed, they went on to found the House of Wessex—from which the current royal family are descended.

By now the Britons must have felt that they had reached the bottom—yet things were to get even worse! In 536 a gigantic volcano eruption, mostly likely in Iceland, led to a ten-year winter of unrelenting misery. The Byzantine historian Procopius wrote how "during the whole year the sun gave forth its light without brightness …. It seemed exceedingly like the sun in eclipse, for the beams it shed were not clear." A second great volcano exploded in 540 and (perhaps) a third in 547, leading to the coldest years in millennia as the sun was faded out by dust. There was widespread famine across Europe; then, just to top it off, the bubonic plague arrived, hitting Constantinople in 542, spreading west and reaching Britain by 544.

In 577 the Saxons reached the Severn Estuary, completing their conquest of southern Britain by cutting the native territory in two. The Britons would now be confined to the modern-day borders of Wales, and to a shrinking corner of the South-West called "West Wales". By the time of Alfred this had been reduced to Kernow, Cornwall in English and home of the "Corn-Welsh", where the native tongue would cling on until the eighteenth century.

The warrior ethic

Although most historians don't like the term, the period following Roman collapse is popularly known as the Dark Ages because of the almost complete absence of contemporary historical records. The first piece of written English dates from AD 450, scratched on stone using the ancient runic alphabet: "This she-wolf is a reward to my kinsman," it says. But almost nothing would be written by the Saxons for another two centuries.

Perhaps the oldest work of art produced by the Anglo-Saxons is a small figurine called "Spong Man", dating to the fifth century and unearthed at a pagan burial site in Norfolk. Carved onto the lid of an urn, he looks like a middle-aged man sat down in his chair contemplating his worries. Another early contribution was the Cerne Abbas Giant, an enormous chalk drawing in Dorset of a happy looking man holding a club and with a huge erection. The statue, which some believed to be an ancient pre-Celtic monument and others to be an early modern prank against Puritans, was only confirmed as eighth century in 2021.[16]

The Anglo-Saxons had eight words for spear, twelve for battle and thirty-six for hero, but before their introduction from Latin they had no concept of table or pillow. Among the oldest words in the English language, dating from this period, include "tits" and "fart", which suggest a society that must have had its moments, but was hardly on the verge of a renaissance.

The newcomers grew oats, rye, and barley, although especially the latter, which they called *bere* and consumed in large quantities. The Anglo-Saxon calendar reflects how closely tied they were to the land. February was *Solmonath*, the month of dirt, "which in that month the English offered cakes" to their gods. April was *Eosturmonath*, "Easter month", after the goddess of spring to whom they made possibly quite cruel offerings; October was *Winterfileth*, or "winter full moon", and after that came *Blotmonath*, or blood month, when the cattle were slaughtered.[17]

There were a limited number of positions open to members of this society, to put it mildly; one could be a warrior, farmer, or slave, and between 10 and 25 per cent of people were unfree, depending on the region (with more in poorer parts of the West). The slaves were probably often native Britons, who would have eventually been integrated into Anglo-Saxon society although not in a very romantic, American Dream-like way. Below the thegns, the aristocracy, were various gradations of peasants; the geneatas, or companions, were the highest caste, direct servants of the thegns, often fighting beside them in battle; then there were cotsetlan, or "cottagers", who would typically spend up to five days a week labouring for their land, while below them were the geburas, often freed slaves or the truly destitute, from which we get the word "boorish".[18]

Old English even had a word, cyrelif, for someone who had entered slavery by choice, because they were so indebted and life was too awful for them to function if free.[19] Above the slaves were the coerls, free peasants, although life probably wasn't that much fun for them, either (the word "churlish", as in sullen and ungrateful, still survives). There must have been class distinctions very early on, as the monk Bede recalls that after a battle in 678 an aristocrat called Imma was captured, and since the aristocratic prisoners were killed or enslaved, pretended to be a mere peasant (although we don't how he carried out this small talk), but was caught out "by his face, dress and speech"; he was sold into slavery.

Life for everyone was pretty grim. At Buckland Cemetery in Kent, corpses from between the years 480 and 750 suggest that while 20 per cent of people died before the age of eighteen, only 6 per cent reached sixty, and "the lucky survivors commonly had dental problems, disabling damage to the joints, badly healed fractures and endemic diseases such as tuberculosis".[20] Childbirth was terrifyingly dangerous and although upper-class women were slightly less likely to die as a result, upper-class men were more likely to die violently than the lower orders.

The Anglo-Saxon social hierarchy was based, as with all societies at the time, on loyalty and reward. A man's obligation was to his lord, a word which derives from *loafward*, literally loaf giver, and this was usually the owner of the land he worked on. Under the Germanic concept of kinship an individual held allegiance to the head of their kin group, at every level: child to father, father to extended family, and to local nobleman. The mutual obligations of giving service and receiving protection and financial support were the bonds that held society together.

In return for service the lord was expected to provide his men with wealth. The Anglo-Saxon poem *The Wanderer*, written around the tenth century but believed to have been composed as early as the seventh, features an exile speaking to his former lord as "gold friend" sitting on a "gift-throne". In the epic *Beowulf* Hrothgar's wife reminds him at one point: "Accept this cup, my loved lord, treasure-giver; O gold-friend of men."

Tiw-day, Woden-day, Thor-day, Frigg-day: the conversion of England

Alfred the Great's Christianity was central to his life, his identity, the reforms he made and his struggle against the heathen Vikings. Although the Danes were a different people, it was largely their religion that separated them from the English; some Saxons went pagan under Danish rule and so in effect became Danes, while Danes who converted stopped being regarded as Vikings. That is why Christian rulers were always trying to get them to accept baptism, even when the Danes were obviously only pretending to convert. Despite this religious element to the conflict, Alfred's kingdom had only been Christian for two centuries, and owed its conversion to a couple of Italians.

The early Anglo-Saxons worshipped the Norse gods, among them the goddess of war, Freyja, who rode a chariot pulled by two cats; her brother Frey the god of peace; and four others whose legacy lasted longer, Tiw, Woden, Thor, and Frigg, giving us the days Tuesday–Friday (Saturday kept its Latin name).[21] They believed they'd go to Valhalla when they died, an afterlife that appears considerably more violent than the Christian heaven, with even children buried with their swords in order to be suitably equipped.[22] Valhalla must also have featured other activities: a grave found at Prittlewell, near Southend, included a sword, shield, spear, camping stool, two drinking vessels, a lyre, and some dice.

Norse paganism had a very dark side, even leaving aside the obvious hostility of Christian chroniclers. The eighth-century monk Bede suggested that in the old days there may have been human sacrifices to Eostre, the Norse goddess of dawn and fertility, so called because the sun rises in the east. Whether Eostre was even a *bona fide* Norse deity is a matter of contention, as we only have Bede's word to rely on, but the name survives in Easter, spring being the time of year when human sacrifices would have taken place in most parts of the world to appease whatever cruel and petty god was in charge of crops. There is certainly plentiful evidence of pre-Christian Scandinavians taking part in human sacrifice, so it's not implausible.

At the other end of the Valhalla pecking order was Weland the Smith, Norse god of ironwork who, like his Greek equivalent Vulcan, was disabled—the only difference being that Weland was deliberately crippled by a king to make him stay in his service. He then murdered the man's son and raped his daughter. If men make their gods in their own image, it certainly doesn't say much for Anglo-Saxon employment practices. But as they spent their days fighting and drinking, the Norse gods can't have known their days would soon be over, at the hands of an urbane, sophisticated, bookworm Jewish God with an overbearing mother.

By the late sixth century Rome, once a city of one million people, had shrunk to a desolate town of a few thousand, in constant fear of invasion and no longer even enjoying basic plumbing—a few decades earlier its aqueducts had been destroyed in the recent wars between the Goths and Byzantines, a final blow to the great city of antiquity. It did, however, have two institutions still functioning: the Church, and a slave market. Under Pope Gregory I, the Church had effectively taken over what was left of the town, establishing it as the western headquarters of Christianity. Rome was just one of five major Christian centres.

Constantinople, the capital of the surviving eastern Roman Empire, was by this point far larger, and also claimed leadership of the Christian world—eventually the two would split in the Great Schism, but this was many centuries ahead. The other three great Christian centres, Jerusalem, Alexandria, and Antioch, would soon fall to Islam, so further strengthening Rome's supreme spiritual position. And it was this Roman version of Christianity which came to shape Alfred's world.

Gregory was a great reformer who is viewed by some historians as a sort of bridge between Late Antiquity and the Middle Ages, the founder of a new and reborn Rome, now a spiritual rather than a military empire. Although a great saint of the Catholic Church, he could be a touch authoritarian; a monk from his monastery once confessed to stealing some coins, so Gregory apparently ordered for him to die alone and his corpse to be thrown on the rubbish pile, as penance for his sins.

One day during the 570s, several years before he became pontiff, Gregory was walking around the marketplace when he spotted a pair of blond-haired pagan slave boys for sale. Thinking it tragic that such innocent-looking children should be ignorant of the Lord, he asked a trader where they came from, and was told they were "Anglii", Angles. Gregory, who was fond of a pun, replied *"Non Angli, sed Angeli"* (not Angles, but angels), a bit of wordplay that still works fourteen centuries later. Not content with this, he asked what region they came from and was told "Deira" (today's Yorkshire). "No," he said, warming to the theme and presumably laughing to himself, *"de ira"*—they are blessed. Impressed with his own punning, Gregory decided that the Angles and Saxons should be shown the true way. (A further embellishment has the pope punning on the name of the king of Deira, Elle, by saying he'd sing "halleluiah" if they were converted, but it seems dubious: how many puns about Dark Ages England can someone make in a row?) The Anglo-Saxons were very fond of wordplay, which features a great deal in their surviving literature; again, without spoiling the story, we probably need to be slightly sceptical about whether Gregory actually said any of this.

The pope ordered a locally based abbot called Augustine to go to Kent to convert the heathens. We can only imagine how Augustine, having enjoyed a relatively nice life at a Benedictine monastery in Rome, must have felt about his new posting to some cold, faraway island populated by shaven-headed savages, and he initially gave up halfway through his trip, leaving his entourage in southern Gaul while he went back to Rome to beg Gregory to call the thing off. At this point Augustine apparently had a dream in which St Peter told him something to the effect that, if he didn't continue his journey, he wouldn't have any need for warm clothes in the afterlife. On he went.

The island must have seemed like an unimaginably grim posting for the priest. Still, in the misery-ridden squalor and obscurity that was sixth-century Britain, Kent was perhaps the least post-apocalyptic, due to its links to the continent. Gaul had been overrun by the Franks in the fifth century, but had basically maintained Roman institutions and culture; the Frankish king Clovis had converted to Catholicism a century before, following relentless pressure from his wife, and then as now people in Britain tended to ape the fashions of those across the water.

The barbarians of Britain were grouped into tribes led by chieftains, the word for their warlords, *cyning*, eventually evolving into its modern usage of "king". There were initially at least twelve small kingdoms, and various smaller tribal groupings, although by Augustine's time a series of hostile takeovers had reduced this to eight—Kent, Sussex, Essex, and Wessex (the West Country and Thames Valley), East Anglia, Mercia (the Midlands), Bernicia (the far North), and Deira (Yorkshire).

Of the other, earlier mini-kingdoms, such as Lindsay (today's Lincolnshire) and Hwicce (Gloucestershire/Worcestershire), we know very little except a confusing list of kings with names like Ethelweard and Ethelherd. When Bernicia and Deira merged into Northumbria the system became known as the Heptarchy, literally the seven realms, one of many aspects of medieval English history that inspired *Game of Thrones*, along with the ceaseless violence. However, it is worth pointing out that like almost everything, this coinage came much later and there might not have been a heptarchy for very long, or any awareness of it at the time.

In 597, when Augustine finally finished his long trip, Kent was ruled by King Ethelbert, supposedly a great-grandson of Hengest. The king of Kent was married to a strong-willed Frankish princess called Bertha, and luckily for Augustine, Bertha was a Christian. She had only agreed to marry Ethelbert on condition that she was allowed to practise her religion, and such was her piety that she kept her own personal bishop.

Bertha persuaded her husband to talk to the missionary, and it's a sign of how suspicious the pagans must have been that at first the king made Augustine stay on the Isle of Thanet, the very same spot where their Jutish ancestors had arrived (now a slightly run-down region of ex-seaside resorts, it was then an island cut off by a channel). The king was perhaps paranoid that the Italian would try to bamboozle him with witchcraft; even when Ethelbert agreed to meet him it had to be under an oak tree, which to the early English had magical properties that could overpower the foreigner's sorcery. (Oak trees had a strong association with religion and mysticism throughout Europe, being seen as the king of the trees and associated with Woden, Zeus, Jupiter, and all the other alpha male gods.)

After being persuaded by his wife, Ethelbert allowed Augustine to baptise 10,000 Kentish men, according to the histories. (This is probably a wild exaggeration; 10,000 is often used as a figure in medieval history, and usually just means "quite a lot of people". It could have been four guys and a dog for all we know.)

Although Ethelbert stood firm in his refusal to convert himself, he let the Christians settle in his capital Canterbury, which thereby became the headquarters of the English Church. Ethelbert told Augustine: "Your words and promises are fair indeed, but they are new and strange to us, and I cannot accept them and abandon the age-old beliefs of the whole English nation." That wasn't enough for Bertha, and eventually she ground him down so that Ethelbert agreed to be baptised, and later that year Augustine became the first primate of England (the title would later be Archbishop of Canterbury).

Various other Christian missionaries would follow St Augustine over to Britain, from southern Europe, North Africa, and the Middle East, going up and down the island teaching the faith, as well as Latin, Greek, art, and literature. For with Christianity came other aspects of Roman civilisation; Ethelbert issued the oldest English coins and was the first Anglo-Saxon king to introduce law codes, a central part of King Alfred's idea of kingship which he was to imitate. Ethelbert's legal code was probably influenced by the Franks, and by his in-laws, who had also introduced something similar around the time. But the Laws of Ethelbert were not only the first works of written English, but also the first laws written in any native European tongue since the fall of Rome, and the first in any Germanic language.

The arrival of Christianity also meant the establishment of schools, and in fact the six oldest continually functioning schools on earth all date back to Anglo-Saxon England, from the King's School Canterbury (597) to newcomer Beverley Grammar School (700).[23] York would also be the first place in Europe to have a cathedral school, the prototype of a university, in the eighth century.

The very first act of written English law deals with theft from Church property, and that was probably because churchmen generally wrote the laws, since they were the only people who could read. It's a sign of how powerful the Church became that under the Laws of Ethelbert's great-great-grandson Wihtred (who ruled from 690 to 725) a bishop's servant receives the same protection as a king's servant, the Church is free from taxation, while there are also fines for "sacrificing to devils". Wihtred's laws also set a fine for priests too drunk to say Mass, which suggests this may have not been an entirely uncommon situation. Curiously, considering the feminist movement at the time was in its infancy, Ethelbert was very progressive in passing a law allowing women to leave their husbands if there was just cause.

But Augustine's work fell apart when Ethelbert died and his half-witted son Eadbald took over and reverted to the old pagan ways, even marrying his stepmother (family values which the Christians disapproved of, although it made financial sense by keeping the inheritance together). Two of the three bishops in England, Mellitus of London and Justus of Rochester, ran off to France, but the other, Lawrence, stood his ground. Luckily Lawrence persuaded the new king to come back on board, convincing him that St Peter had physically attacked him because the king had forsaken God. Eadbald, afraid for his friend's safety, dumped his wife/stepmother, who had in the meantime gone insane, as a monk recorded with some glee.

Augustine didn't do so well with the native Britons. When they arrived to meet him a few years later, he didn't get up from his chair, and they took this for arrogance, although this is probably a very simple explanation for something more complicated. The Britons had been Christian, and largely independent from Rome, for some time and probably resented the idea of the religious leader of the Saxons, who had been Christian for about five minutes, explaining Christianity to them. As a result there developed a huge dispute between the Celtic and English Churches which was sort of resolved when the king of Northumbria, Ethelfrith the Ferocious, killed a load of monks.

Ethelbert's sister had married the king of Essex, perhaps the weakest of the seven kingdoms, and their son allowed the Christians to settle in his capital, Lundenwic, where they built a church in honour of St Paul, close to the site of Lud Hill, a place with ancient religious significance. Ethelbert's daughter Ethelberga, meanwhile, had married Edwin, king of Northumbria, the northern kingdom which was now undergoing one of the most remarkable cultural revivals of European history—a "Northumbrian renaissance" which would produce one of the most important thinkers not just in English history, but in any history.

CHAPTER 3

The world of Beowulf: Northumbrian golden age

In August 1939 archaeologists made one of the greatest discoveries in British history at a spot called Sutton Hoo in Suffolk. It had long been rumoured that the area, which featured lots of old clearly man-made mounds, had some association with ancient kings. John Dee, who was Elizabeth I's advisor/wizard-in-residence during the sixteenth century, had tried digging around the area; a century later, in 1690, a crown had been found but, annoyingly for historians, melted down.

In 1926 a Colonel Pretty and his wife had moved into a local estate which came with the mounds, and after the colonel's death his widow became more interested in the idea that they might be burial mounds, even hiring a psychic to prove it. In 1939 she hired a self-taught archaeologist Basil Brown to dig it up—and what he and his team found in the late summer of that year was a glimpse into what is sometimes called "the heroic age". Inside was a longboat, in the centre of which was a wooden chamber with a helmet and sword, some spears, a battle axe, a shield decorated with birds and dragons, drinking horns in silver, a silver bowl from Byzantium, ten shallow silver bowls, some more bowls, spoons, a gold buckle, a huge purse, nineteen pieces of jewelry and forty coins from France.[24] A cauldron was attached to a chain measuring 3.75 metres, which must have hung from rafters and looked very impressive.

It was one of the most amazing discoveries in British history but, unfortunately, people were for some reason rather distracted in August 1939 and maybe didn't want to be reminded about a previous, highly successful German invasion of Britain.

Sutton Hoo's burial mound dates from the seventh century, a time when Suffolk was part of the kingdom of East Anglia, and the burial site contains both pagan and Christian objects, which suggests that the kings were hedging their bets. Despite being a burial site there's no actual body, although they later found an empty coffin, and it's probable that an East Anglian king was laid to rest here. The best-known monarch of the time was Redwald, from a dynasty called the Wuffingas, after their founder, Wuffa, who may have come from Sweden originally, and the famous helmet found at Sutton Hoo (in fact just a few fragments) has come to be associated with him. After Ethelbert of Kent, Redwald of East Anglia was the next king to be seen as *bretwalda*; he was regarded as a great king, as he won some important battles, but not much else is known of him.

Despite this exciting find, it was in the most northerly of the kingdoms where Anglo-Saxon England first began to flourish. Northumbria—the Humber River traditionally marks the start of the north of England—arose out of two smaller kingdoms, Deira and Bernicia, a union that came about through the joining of two not very happy families. King Ethelfrith of Bernicia, known as "the Ferocious" perhaps because he wiped out a party of monks who'd turned up for peace negotiations, had united the two realms after he married the queen of Deira and killed her father; he also attempted to kill her brother Edwin, who fled first to Wales and then to East Anglia. Apart from that the marriage seemed to be happy.

As well as fighting family members, Ethelfrith was also locked in constant wars with the various Anglo-Saxon, British, and Gaelic-speaking peoples to the west and north. Before Alfred laid down the rudimentary workings of a state, the Dark Ages economy relied mainly on cattle rustling and capturing metal from opponents in battle; there was no way of building up the state through any sort of economy so the measure of a king's worth was how much he could beat his neighbours in futile wars, until eventually he was killed by someone else (the main difference with the arrival of Christianity at first was that the Church got one-third of the booty). Of six East Anglian kings living around the time of Sutton Hoo, five died violently and the other's fate remains a mystery.

One ruler of this period, Penda of Mercia, killed three East Anglian kings in a row, before the fourth decided it was better to side with him, only to get himself killed in battle.

Ethelfrith had somehow persuaded Redwald to kill Edwin, then hiding with the East Anglians, but during his darkest hours a stranger came to the Northumbrian exile warning him to flee, and by later accounts this saviour was revealed to be Paulinus of York, another Italian churchman. Paulinus had been brought over by Edwin's Kentish Christian wife Ethelberga, daughter of Ethelbert and Bertha, and must have been wondering what on earth he'd done to end up in this place.

Instead of killing Edwin, however, Redwald had been persuaded by *his* wife (an adamant pagan) to spare his life, and so instead the two men marched north and killed Ethelfrith, with Edwin taking the throne.

Edwin was unsure about signing up to this strange new religion, and so held a council to debate the matter, the main focus of the debate being whether the old gods had favoured them in battle. The man–god relationship in pagan times could be openly superficial, with men worshipping deities on account of what they brought to the relationship, and dumping them if they were thought responsible for military defeat or a poor harvest, or if they just found a more fashionable god. After the leaders had debated the matter for a while, a humble counsellor perked up with these words:

"The present life of man, O King, seems to me, like the swift flight of a sparrow through the room wherein you sit at supper in winter, with your companions, and a good fire in the midst, while the storms of rain and snow prevail outside. The sparrow, I say, flying in at one door and immediately out at another, whilst he is within is safe from the wintry storm; but after a short space of fair weather, he immediately vanishes out of your sight into the dark winter from whence he had emerged. So this life of man appears for a short space, but of what went before, or what is to follow, we know nothing. Therefore, if this new teaching has brought any more certain knowledge, it seems only right that we should follow it."

As described by Bede, it remains one of the most moving passages from Old English, and is certainly more impressive than Ethelbert's reason for converting, which seems to have been simply to please his wife and have an easier life.

The most enthusiastic convert seemed to be the pagan high priest Coifi, who asked if he could lead a twenty-mile procession to the pagan temple and desecrate it by throwing a spear into the gods' sanctuary, which he did, much to the bafflement of onlookers who wondered if he had lost his marbles. Coifi's rather childish gripe was that he wasn't paid as much as his contemporaries, which he blamed not on the king but on the gods, proving there are few things more dangerous than an embittered employee, even for an immortal.

Although Edwin certainly allowed Christianity to take root, he seemed to have been quite ambiguous in his own beliefs. His wife tried her best to convert him, with the encouragement of Pope Boniface V, who told her to "persevere with all your might to soften his hard heart", giving her a silver mirror and gilded ivory comb as encouragement.

Bede exaggerated when he said of Edwin that "Like none of the Angles before him he held under his sway the whole of Britain, both the Anglian kingdoms and those of the Britons as well." This hyperbole led later writers of the period to include Edwin among a list of overkings termed as *bretwaldas*, which translates as "wide ruler", although it came to mean "ruler of Britain". This begins with Aelle of Sussex in the late fifth century and includes Ethelbert before concluding with Alfred, but there wasn't any institutional power as such. There was no "high king" of the Anglo-Saxons, only a perpetual competition between rival kingdoms whose borders might shift every time someone got a sword stuck in them.

Edwin went on to rule a largely peaceful kingdom, even if it inevitably ended with his violent death, in a battle with the Mercians. It was such a golden age that, according to the monk Bede, "in the days of Edwin a woman with a baby at her breast might have travelled over the island without suffering an insult" (he may have been a bit rose tinted about that—crime rates at the time would have been absurdly high, and anyone travelling in groups of less than thirty could expect something terrible to happen to them). It was also noted that Edwin built drinking fountains across the highways of his realm, so that travellers could have water during their relaxing journey through the kingdom.

Traces of Edwin's hall in Yeavering were discovered in the mid-twentieth century; the site consisted of around ten buildings, including one which the archaeologist described as being an example of "strange incompetence" and designed to be rectangular but ending up as a rhomboid; after it fell down, another was built in its place, which also had wonky walls. After the Romans, pagan Anglo-Saxon England must have seemed quite desolate.

The Northumbrian kings had another seat, at Bamburgh on the North Sea coast; this Bamburgh castle would be destroyed by the Vikings and rebuilt by the Normans, before being restored by eccentric Victorian industrialist William Armstrong, who had made his money by inventing the hydraulic crane and modern artillery. It has since been used in multiple films, including most recently the 2015 *Macbeth* and *The Last Kingdom*. If you've seen a medieval-y looking castle by a beach in a film, it's probably Bamburgh.

Even if they could design a comfy palace in which to relax, kings rarely got much time to do anything before being fatally wounded anyway. After Redwald's death his son Eorpwald embraced Christianity fully, and for his troubles was murdered by subjects in 627. Four years later his half-brother Sigibert took the throne and became a Christian, but was then killed in 637 by his cousin Anna (a man). King Penda of Mercia then killed Anna and gave the kingdom to Anna's brother Ethelhere; Ethelhere and Penda were then killed in 654 at the battle of Winwed near Leeds, the first great battle of note in Saxon England; this involved the armies of four different kingdoms, and a frightening number of odd-sounding barbarians slaughtering each other. Though records of this period are shaky, the scribes record that only two princes on the losing side escaped that day, including Cadfael ("battle-dodger"), one of the less impressively nicknamed early kings. His escape is self-explanatory.

All the Anglo-Saxon kingdoms were dominated by the never-ending violent struggles between various warlords; battles were frequent, and just as likely to involve two factions from within a kingdom. Far from being great Edward G Robinson events, many of these fights involved as few as fifty or sixty men on each side, although Penda of Mercia's force may have been several thousand strong. *Here* was the name given to an army (related to *Wehr* in German, as in *Wehrmacht*), and by the laws of King Ine a *here* was considered anything over thirty-five men, so the battles of the age were very small affairs, rather like fights outside pubs in English town centres.

To get some impression of what these scenes would have looked like it's worth knowing that during this pre-Christian period people's faces were often painted or tattooed, men and women dyed their hair, with men going for blue, green, and orange locks, while everyone wore gold bracelets, as did the Vikings later.

After Edwin's death the different parts of Northumbria split once again, and Ethelfrith's son Eanfrith ruled Bernicia, the people reverting to the "abominations" of paganism in Bede's words, whatever that means. Paulinus fled, leaving another Italian, James the Deacon, all alone to run an isolated church in the wilds of Deira. Luckily Northumbrian kings never lasted long, and Eanfrith was no exception; he had made a truce with the local British chieftain Cadwallon but after falling out with him he went off with twelve soldiers to negotiate peace. It's not recorded what they talked about but by the end of the meeting Eanfrith was dead.

He was replaced by his brother Oswald, who once again united Deira and Bernicia after defeating Cadwallon. Since his uncle Edwin probably wanted him dead, Oswald had grown up in exile in the Gaelic-speaking region in what is now the west of Scotland, along with his younger brothers Osguid, Oswiu, Oslac, Oslaph and Offa (Anglo-Saxons had the habit of giving their children names all starting with the same letter). There he had converted to Christianity, probably more sincerely than Edwin, and went one better than his uncle by becoming an actual saint.

Bede says of Oswald that although he wielded supreme power over the whole island, he was always wonderfully humble, kind, and generous to the poor and to strangers. But Oswald earned his sainthood by firmly establishing the faith in his kingdom, asking his Irish contacts to lend him a bishop; the first one they sent was apparently too austere, so instead they dispatched St Aidan with Oswald, who spoke Gaelic, acting as his interpreter. Aidan went on to establish churches all over Northumbria and probably did more even than Augustine in making England Christian.

The Irish played a huge part in maintaining and then spreading Christianity in the West, especially through the monasteries. Monasticism had begun in Egypt in the fourth century with St Anthony the Great, a holy man from Alexandria who fled to the desert to escape the attention of adoring intellectuals and other pseuds, his fans rather annoying him. Instead, the city folk followed him to his hermit's cave, and then to the desert, and realising he'd never escape from them he established a community of hermits. And so the first monastery, St Anthony's, was created and by the fifth century there were 700 around the eastern Mediterranean.

Monasticism thrived in remote and inhospitable regions, and the idea really picked up in Ireland soon after the country was converted to Christianity by St Patrick in the fifth century. Irish monks, in particular, loved the austerity and self-inflicted misery associated with the religious life, and the country's harsh environment provided the perfect backdrop;

the most extreme was Skellig Michael, off the coast of Co. Kerry, an isolated mountain island that is absurdly dangerous to reach and climb up and can only be accessed on calm days. Once there, you'll be totally isolated and have only puffins and Luke Skywalker for company.[25] There seemed to be some competition among Irish clerics to find the most inconvenient and uncomfortable place to settle down in, to show how holy they were, but isolated places also had the advantage of being safe; if you found it hard and dangerous to get somewhere, so will the Vikings.

In doing so Irish monks helped to preserve many of the ancient texts. So devoted were they to the written word that they even had wars about monastic books, of all things; in one debacle, called the Battle of the Book, which took place in the kingdom of Cairbre Drom Cliabh in north-west Ireland between 555 and 561, two clans went to war after St Columba had illegally copied a version of the Psalms belonging to St Finnian, most likely the only war to ever begin over copyright infringement. The battle between the two groups led to "thousands" of deaths.[26]

And now it was Christianised Northumbria, under Irish influence, which produced England's first great literary flourishing. Among the many surviving gems from this period are the Lindisfarne gospels, a multicoloured masterpiece made at a time when most books only used three colours, laboriously written and illustrated in the Irish style by a monk called Eadfrith, between 698 and 721. (Eadfrith was apparently also the first man to use a lead pencil.[27]) The Lindisfarne gospels are in Latin but in 970 a monk called Aldred added an English translation, making it the oldest English gospels.[28]

There was also the *Codex Amiatinus*, a gigantic Bible made at Jarrow but taken to Rome as a gift in 716 by St Ceolfrith, an enormous undertaking that killed him. To make matters worse, this oldest surviving Bible in Latin ended up in Florence where the frontispiece dedication to "Ceolfrith of the English" was erased and replaced with "Peter of the Lombards"—a great act of plagiarism that was uncovered only in modern times.

Then there is the St Cuthbert Gospel, a pocket-sized Bible found in the coffin of one of the holiest men of the age, a man who would play a significant part in Alfred's story and the creation of England; indeed, he even went on to become the first dead person recognised as head of state.[29]

Born in 634 in Dunbar, in what is now Scotland, Cuthbert became a monk in 651 after seeing a vision of St Aidan on the night he died and became a noted aesthetic who "only seemed to eat raw onions and the eggs of seabirds, and would stand on the shore for hours knee-deep in prayer and freezing sea-water."[30] Later he would become prior of Lindisfarne, a monastery built on a tidal island by St Aidan and which would become a thriving and rich community by the Viking age.

Yet one story from Cuthbert's life illustrates just how unpopular the new religion was with some people. On one occasion some local Northumbrian men were jeering at monks drowning in a river, and when Cuthbert asked why he was told that "for they have robbed people of their old ways of worship, and how the new worship is to be conducted, nobody knows". Inevitably, as happens with these early medieval tales written by monks, God now intervened with a gust of wind and the monks were saved.

It was around this point there arrived one of the most remarkable figures of the period, Theodore of Canterbury; born in Syria to a Greek family, Theodore had gone to Rome in his late fifties, which was extraordinary in itself, but then, aged sixty-six, he was sent off to run the Anglo-Saxon Church, without any knowledge of their language. The position had become available after the previous Archbishop of Canterbury, an unfortunate Wighard, had travelled to Rome in AD 667 in order to be consecrated by the pope, and almost immediately died of plague after a journey taking weeks. Theodore was only given the job because everyone else refused it, and so they just nominated the Syrian guy.

Theodore had been taught a classical Greek education in Constantinople, and for someone raised in the antique culture of the Hellenic world, Britain must have seemed like something from *Conan the Barbarian*. But despite his lack of knowledge of the place, Theodore stayed for twenty-two years, totally reorganising the English Church. He was not the only churchman to make such a long journey; with him came Hadrian, a North African who became abbot of St Augustine's Abbey in Canterbury, and who lived for forty years in his new home. At the General Synod in Hertford in 672 Theodore "was the first of the archbishops whom the whole Anglo-Saxon Church consented to obey", in the words of Bede.

The Christian religion introduced the Anglo-Saxons to a more sophisticated Mediterranean world, and exposure to the Roman culture that their primitive forefathers had ignored. Latin words entered the language for the first time, and some people began to read. Previously the Saxons had used the runic alphabet, which was rather limited; for example, it had nothing to signify the "g" sound, and there were no spaces between words, so reading anything longer than a short list of who killed whom is maddeningly difficult.

Among the other great holy men of the time was Chad, appointed as bishop of Mercia by Theodore, and a man so holy his boss found it irritating. Chad was so holy he refused to ride a horse, and when Theodore demanded that he use one, because it would take days otherwise to get to their destination, Chad refused so the sixty-nine-year-old Syrian archbishop heaved him into the saddle.

Yet not everyone favoured the aesthete's life of walking or eating raw onions. Cuthbert's contemporary St Wilfred, who succeeded Chad as Bishop of Northumbria, fell out with Northumbria's king partly because he liked to surround himself with warriors while feasting and drinking, and also hiring masons from the continent to build a new church of stone at a time when kings' halls were made from wood. Wilfred's new church in Hexham was built using 7,000 tonnes of recycled Roman material from across the Tyne Valley. Out of the ruins of one Roman civilisation, another was being built. But this church also proved his ruin.

Northumbria's king Ecgfrith, son of Oswiu, had been married to a woman called Aethelthyrth, who refused to sleep with him. The king asked for Wilfred's help, but after his intervention she became a nun. She rewarded him by giving him land in Hexham for his church, but the king was (obviously) furious.

Ecgfrith now married a woman called Iurminburh who turned him against Wilfred, the bishop's biographer describing her as a jezebel and she-wolf. Wilfred's biographer, Stephen of Ripon, also claimed that he never drank too much "and that there were plenty of witnesses who would vouch for this", which suggests that he might in fact have drunk too much.

Wilfred was exiled to Francia for three years but had a much better time in a country where bishops were expected to live in grand palaces and have lots of expensive wine, and had far more secular power (indeed they could lead armies). However, once again he fell out with the queen, in this case Bathilde, wife of Clovis II, and had to come back. However, in Wessex he had to leave once again because of the king's wife, sister of the same Iurminburh and ended up in Sussex, the last pagan kingdom in England, and played a part in its final submission to Christianity. Here, according to his ever loyal biographer, he brought rain to end a drought and converted large numbers of heathens, "some freely and some at the king's command". In alliance with Mercia, Wilfred persuaded Sussex's King Ethelwealh to convert.

Unfortunately, at this point a rogue aristocrat from Wessex called Cedwalla turns up, kills the king and decides to invade the Isle of Wight, killing its ruler and capturing his two brothers. Wilfred seemed to have gone along with Cedwalla on the agreement that he give Christianity a try, and when the warlord had his two captives executed he allowed them to convert. Here Bede tries to persuade his readers that the two young men went happily to their deaths "assured of their entry into the eternal kingdom". I bet they were delighted by the day's events.

And so the old religion died out across the island.

Pope Gregory had declared that pagans should be tolerated, but the Christian rulers inevitably began persecuting them as soon as possible; a surviving manifesto states, "If any witch, or wizard, or false swearer, or worshipper of the dead, or any foul contaminated, manifest whore, be anywhere in the land, men shall drive them out." Archbishop Theodore of Canterbury's *Penitential*, which was written after he died in the year 690 close to his nineteeth birthday, gives us some idea of the strange things people got up to in the old pagan days, among the punishments described being "If any woman puts her daughter on the roof or into an oven to cure a fever, she shall do seven years' penance."[31]

The Christians also banned the traditional Saxon custom of worshipping stones, or of "burning grain to preserve the purity of a house with a corpse in it". There had also been some sort of animal-worship going on before, since Paulinus ordered a youth to shoot down a crow from a tree to prove to "those who were still bound ... to heathenism" not to idolise birds.

But rather than banning them outright, the Christians co-opted some of the pagan traditions, so that the festival of Christ's death kept the name Eostre, and the new churches were built on old pagan sites; many religious grounds dating back to pre-Celtic times can boast a continuous history of worship encompassing Stone Age, Roman and Saxon paganism, Catholicism, Protestantism, and Irish theme pub. (The degree to which Christian festivals are copied from pagan rituals is, however, hugely exaggerated in the popular understanding.) And some hangovers from pagan times still exist today: The Boar's Head carol, sung every year at Queen's College, Oxford by a procession carrying a boar's head, almost certainly dates back to an early Anglo-Saxon offering to Freyja.

Some rulers hedged their bets; Redwald, a man self-confident enough to claim descent from Caesar, didn't abandon paganism altogether because he was scared of his wife. Instead, the king had two shrines built next to each other, one for Christ and one for the old gods. (Which, no doubt, the God of the Old Testament would understand, famously not being jealous.)

Bede

Most of what we know of this time, and it was hardly a period of rolling news, comes from the Venerable Bede, a monk from Northumbria who spent almost his entire life in a monastery and yet was, without question, the greatest historian of the age (he was also, it has to be said, pretty much the only one).

Born in 672 in Wearmouth, now part of the city of Sunderland, Bede was orphaned as a child, and at the age of twelve was sent to the nearby monastery at Jarrow in today's Co. Durham. Things didn't get off to a good start—a year later, in 686, some local villagers arrived looking for parsley, optimistically hoping that this might cure them of the plague. They infected the whole monastery, and when the disease had left, only Bede and the elderly abbot were alive; however, not to be put off by this staffing shortage, they continued the chanting as a duo.

Life in the monastery would have been gruelling, with most of the monks' time spent laboriously writing and copying ancient writings from dawn until dark, in conditions so cold that the quills would turn to ice and slip out of their hands, Dark Ages monasteries in Northumbria not being heated (obviously). Making and writing a book was tediously laborious at the time, the pages made from calves' skin (and taking 500 of the animals to make a Bible). And yet Bede managed to write sixty-eight books, on subjects including philosophy, astronomy, grammar, and mathematics. So quickly had Northumbria progressed since the arrival of Christianity that Bede had access to 200 books, mostly from Italy, more than either Oxford or Cambridge had at the start of the Tudor period seven centuries later.[32]

Bede's great book *The Ecclesiastical History of the English Nation*, written in Latin some time around 731, was not only the first history of the Anglo-Saxons, but the first reference to an English nation, rather than a collection of tribal fiefdoms.[33] Because Bede was an Angle, he called the people the English, although it might just as easily have been Saxony, and was called *Saxonia* in Latin in some cases; just as Celtic languages still use names for their neighbours derived from Saxon, Finns still refer to the Germans as "Saska").

Considering the circumstances, Bede expressed a perhaps mindlessly undeserved sense of national confidence, referring to the English as "God's destined race"; although why God would put his destined race on a rainswept island in the middle of nowhere is anyone's guess.

He also suggested that God himself gave them the land, justifying this logic with the argument that the Britons had invoked the Almighty's ire by failing to convert the Anglo-Saxon newcomers—as if asking, "Have you ever thought about Jesus?" to some marauding barbarian maniac would have done much good.

As well as history, he also recorded news from all over the country, even from far-off Sussex, where the South Saxons were reported jumping off a cliff during a terrible famine—at Beachy Head, still the most popular suicide spot in the country. Bede's work was copied and sent around the country, the first time that men from the different kingdoms read about the rest of the island, but it was Alfred who had it translated from Latin into English.

Bede's legacy stretched further still. Europeans at the time dated the years using twenty-eight different methods, the most popular being from the foundation of Rome (731 BC), or from the start of a monarch's reign, a difficult task when there were seven or more English kings at any one time and their life expectancy tended to be quite short. Pious Bede thought it was more appropriate to measure from Christ's birth, an idea that had first been put forward by a Greek called Dennis the Little; thanks to Bede the terms Before Christ and *Anno Domini* (year of our lord) were popularised and soon the system was used all across Christendom (unfortunately Dennis was a few years out, and Jesus was probably born in 4 BC, but Bede can hardly be blamed for that). Not bad considering where he was, or that he was blind for most of his life, so blind that on one occasion he was tricked into saying Mass to an empty church by some monk pranksters.

After a lifetime of work, on the evening of May 25, 735 Bede dictated while a young monk, Wilbert, wrote down his words as instructed. At one point Bede said: "It is well finished. Now raise my head in your hands." Then he died. He worked, literally to the last minute, and was buried in Durham Cathedral, where the Latin inscription "Here lie the venerable bones of Bede" were mistranslated into "Here lie the bones of the venerable Bede," giving him the slightly odd name he has since been known by since.

Bede epitomised the Northumbrian golden age, a glorious eruption of light in one of the remotest part of the continent. It was a flame of literacy, and civilisation, that would become threatened by the violence and destruction of the Viking Age.

CHAPTER 4

Return of the kings: from Oswald to Offa

King Oswald, who had gone by the rather exaggerated title "emperor of all Britain", died fighting the Mercians in 642, and power passed to his brother Oswiu, who struggled to keep together the various factions in the kingdom. Oswald, having fallen in battle with pagans, was soon hailed as a saint; before his burial, a beam of light was seen coming out of his grave. His cult spread across northern Europe, and his image is found on various old churches in Germany as well as England. His head was taken to Durham cathedral and his arms ended up in Peterborough for some reason; a second head of Oswald's turned up in Frisia, where it was reverently received apparently without scepticism,[34] while others were found in Luxemburg, Switzerland, and Germany. As none of his contemporaries mentioned him having five heads—which probably would have been the first thing a casual observer mentioned—we can be fairly sure they aren't all authentic.

Meanwhile his successor Oswiu was a keen convert who sent clergymen all over England and forced King Sigeberht of Essex to build St Peter's at Bradwell-on-the-Sea in 653, the oldest surviving Anglo-Saxon building, and built by St Chad's brother, the equally holy St Cedd.

Oswiu's great achievement was to establish Whitby Abbey, appointing his cousin Hilda as abbess. Hilda, as a thirteen year old, had been among those baptised under King Edwin's instructions in 627, but when in 633 Penda of Mercia overran the kingdom she was taken by Paulinus to Kent. Many years later, aged thirty-three, she returned to Northumbria to become a nun and now, five years later, assumed a more senior role. Hilda died at the age of sixty-six, having spent seven years suffering from a fever, but under her rule Whitby had become hugely important as a place of learning.

It was here that Oswiu held a famous synod that decided the most contentious issues dividing the Church in Britain, among them the dating of Easter (still a source of never-ending dispute in Christianity) and what haircuts monks should have; it was so contentious that some of the monks, such as those at Lindisfarne, stormed out of the conference and refused to accept the rulings.

The divide was essentially between practices established by the Church in Rome and those which had developed among Celtic Churches, for several centuries cut off from the continental mainstream. But there were also divisions with the Greek-speaking half of the Church, and indeed Theodore had been given a chaperone by the pope to ensure that he didn't introduce any weird Greek stuff in his new home. Theodore even had to wait four months for his hair to grow before he could go, because he had an eastern-style monk's tonsure which was now frowned upon in the West.

The dispute over the timing of Easter is an issue that still divided Christianity, and at the time the Celtic and Roman Churches were at odds. No doubt the Celtic representatives, who had a far older Christian tradition than the Saxons, resented that the newcomers now represented the more powerful and mainstream church body, but the Anglo-Saxons themselves were divided, with Northumbria heavily influenced by Celtic tradition. Indeed, for two decades Oswiu and his half-Kentish wife Eanfled had celebrated Easter at different times because they came from different traditions, stubbornly celebrating at different weekends.

During this great dispute, Wilfred made a rational and perhaps unanswerable appeal to his fellow countrymen, asking them: "Do you think that a handful of people in a corner of the remotest island is to be preferred to the universal Church of Christ which is spread through the world?" To which a reasonable and moderate Englishman would obviously answer "Yes".

The Roman delegation was not helped by the fact that Wessex's King Cenwalh turned up with his Frankish bishop, Agilbert, who had made no effort to learn Saxon, and the Saxon king knew no Frankish, and the two men couldn't get on, an early example of nascent Anglo-French co-operation at its best. Yet the universal, Catholic argument prevailed, as it was inevitably going to.

The growth of monasteries was a central part of Anglo-Saxon England's development. Since there were no universities for another 400 years, most cerebral activity took place in monasteries, where men and women could learn the classics and the Bible. Whitby was an example of a double monastery, with nuns and monks in separate chambers, an idea banned for most of the later medieval period for probably obvious reasons, and someone like Hilda was able to wield power in a way women couldn't many centuries later.

During Hilda's time a shy monk at Whitby by the name of Caedmon wrote the first English poems, indeed really the first English of any sort, explaining the myth of creation, turning words into poetry like a cow turns grass into dung, as one contemporary said (it was meant as a compliment). *Caedmon's Hymn* was written sometime between AD 660 and 680, and features the lines "Then the Guardian of Mankind adorned this middle-earth below, the world for men, Everlasting Lord, Almighty King." If this all sounds vaguely familiar, it is because J. R. R. Tolkien, who wrote *The Lord of the Rings* and *The Hobbit*, was an Anglo-Saxon scholar. Indeed King Oswald, of five-heads fame, was cited by J. R. R. Tolkien as an inspiration for Aragorn, the returning king in his epic, and the people of Rohan are how Tolkien imagined the Anglo-Saxons, down to their names and lifestyles, with Théoden living in a great hall.

The most famous early work of Old English, however, is *Beowulf*, which was written down between 680 and 800, although it is far older as an oral tale. It is set in Scandinavia, the old country as it was then, at around the time of the Anglo-Saxon invasion of Britain, and is the most precise surviving guide to the culture of the very early English. Indeed, its one apparent link to real history is the hero's uncle, King Hygelac, who some historians believe to be the same man identified as invading Frisia around AD 523.

Beowulf tells of a warrior who kills a monster called Grendel, then kills its mother at the bottom of a lake, then returns home and kills a dragon. Then dies. Beowulf is a Geat, a tribe from southern Sweden, and goes to Denmark to help King Hrothgar of the Scyldings, whose great hall Heorot has been occupied by Grendel these past twelve years. The hero is a Christian and the poem was written after the Angles had converted but it clearly dates to a period before Christianity, and a heroic time of warriors when men were driven by fate—*wyrd*—from which we get the modern English "weird". It's almost melancholy in lamenting the loss of a far more violent past, the good old days when men were men, before the Christians stopped people fighting monsters or putting their daughters in ovens. Beowulf may even be a metaphor for the end of human sacrifice.

Having killed the "loathsome creature", Beowulf's life ends in failure, with his country overrun anyway. The ultimate conclusion of the poem is that all the fame Beowulf won in life is meaningless.

Christianisation barely made any difference to the endless cycle of violence at the top of society. Northumbria's Oswiu was succeeded by his brother Osred, most famous for going around the convents of his kingdom groping nuns. After that came Oswiu's son, the hugely obscure Eadfrith (670–685), who perhaps invented the silver penny, the world's oldest surviving currency; his reign, however, came to a speedy conclusion when he went to do battle with the Picts at Forfar. He wasn't the only one to meet a grisly end. During its golden age Northumbria had sixteen kings in 100 years, and only three died peacefully on the throne; two were exiled, five deposed, three killed in battle, and two murdered. The war between the two main rival clans continued throughout and was only resolved in 867 when the Vikings adjudicated, by killing both claimants.

An intriguing glimpse into the world of Beowulf came about in 2009 when a man called Terry Herbert discovered what became called the "Staffordshire hoard" near Lichfield, a vast trove of 4,600 items of gold, silver, and other precious metals, featuring swords, rings, crosses, and other treasures. Most exciting, however, at least if you're into that sort of thing, is that we might know whose treasure it was.

Northumbria was already starting to lose its dominance, the most powerful of the Anglo-Saxon monarchs now being Penda of Mercia, an almost unbeatable warrior who was never included among the list of Bretwalda by Bede perhaps because of his paganism. Mercia roughly corresponds to the Midlands, and the name translates at the boundary, being the boundary with the British—but Mercia is the Latin term and its people would have called it "the Mark".

Penda had consistently won battles to an extent that, in 655, so Bede wrote, the Northumbrians were forced to hand over a large peace offering, with Oswiu "exposed to the savage and insupportable attacks of Penda", forced "to promise him an incalculable and incredible store of royal treasures and gifts as the price of peace, on condition that Penda would return home and cease to devastate, or rather utterly destroy, the kingdoms under his rule". This store of treasure, many historians believe, is what Terry Herbert discovered over thirteen centuries later.

Penda was eventually, and inevitably, killed in battle (as a basic rule Mercia and Northumbria were always at war) and afterwards the Northumbrians installed his son, the unfortunately named Paeda, as a puppet; however, Paeda was soon murdered, possibly by his wife, and his brother Wulfhere was put on the throne. Wulfhere converted to Christianity and this seemed to pacify the place a little bit, or at any rate the existence of monasteries gave unpopular kings somewhere to go when it all got too difficult; his immediate successors, Ethelred and Coenred, both retired to religious houses.

Mercia continued to rise and in 748 King Ethelbald (716–757) was recognised as *rex Sutanglorum*, king of the southern English; Ethelbald was a famous letch, a violator of men's wives and also "the brides of Christ", and holy man Boniface berated Ethelbald for his lifestyle, stating that the king had never taken a wife because he was "governed by lust". Eventually his behaviour led his own bodyguard to stab him to death. That same year in Wessex, King Sigeberht was deposed by the Witan, the ruling council, for his "unjust acts" and then outlawed to the Weald of Kent where a swineherd stabbed him to death in a blood feud.

Ethelbald's second cousin Offa then murdered Ethelbald's successor Beornred a few weeks later and took the throne, Asser later writing: "There was in fairly recent times a certain warlike king called Offa, who terrified all the neighbouring kings and princes around him, and who had a great dyke built between Wales and Mercia, from sea to sea." Offa is still best remembered for the ditch he built to stop the Welsh entering his kingdom; Offa's Dyke is still, give or take a few miles, the modern boundary between England and Wales, and the physical remains are in place, just about.

Offa reigned for forty years, becoming the most powerful of early Anglo-Saxon kings and a model for Alfred. During his reign Offa conquered the smaller kingdoms of Sussex and Kent, and through extending to the English Channel he seems to have been hugely influenced by the more civilised, Roman-influenced kingdom of the Franks.

The Franks had been the first of the western barbarians to adopt Catholic Christianity, after God had helped King Clovis during a particularly tricky battle against another German tribe, the Allemani in 496.[i] But in the late eighth century Charlemagne was the first of the barbarian kings to really bring western Europe out of the Dark Ages, doing much to encourage literature and the arts and, more importantly, killing lots of people who got in his way; however, after slaughtering 4,500 Saxon noblemen for refusing to convert, Charles the Great mellowed in his old age, abolishing the death penalty for paganism.

Charlemagne's father Pepin had made himself king after deposing the descendants of Clovis, and having himself crowned by bishops, perhaps the first time a coronation took on its modern, religious nature. Charlemagne went one further by having himself crowned emperor in 800, setting the way for the kingdom of the Franks to become France (although the Frankish rulers continued to speak a form of German for another 200 years). He also made his court a centre of learning, employing perhaps the greatest Anglo-Saxon scholar of the age, Alcuin of York. In total more than 300 of Alcuin's letters have survived, many relating to his homeland; he wrote many grovelling things about King Offa when he was alive and some rather less flattering things after he had died.

Offa and Charlemagne corresponded by letter and exchanged gifts, although the emperor's were noticeably better. In 796 the Frankish ruler sent a missive, calling Offa his "dearest brother", "strong protector of your earthly country", and "defender of the holy faith". The only other surviving correspondence from the ruler of the Franks is a letter written later that year, in which Charlemagne complains about his Anglo-Saxon counterpart selling him poor-quality cloaks and blankets.[35] "What's the use of these little bits of cloth," he wrote. "I can't cover myself with them when I'm in bed, I can't protect myself against the wind and rain when I'm riding, and when I get down to answer a call of nature, I suffer because my legs are frozen."

The two monarchs also agreed for Charlemagne's son to marry Offa's daughter, but when the Mercian insisted that his son marry one of the Frank's daughters as part of the bargain, Charlemagne shut all Frankish ports to him; a no, in other words.

---

[i] The tribe's name survives in the French word for Germany, Allemagne.

His new links to Francia seemed to give Offa ideas. He began to mint coins at Canterbury with his face on them, in the Roman style, showing the king "with elaborately dressed hair arranged in curls, cut to give hints of light and shade" while "on others he is diademed and draped like a Roman emperor, and is also shown wearing rich jewels".[36] Offa's wife Cynethryth was the only Anglo-Saxon queen to ever appear on a coin, although this probably reflects less his love of a good woman than a growing pretention about copying the Roman emperors, the small Mercian kingdom imitating imperial styles. Indeed, one coin from the period has *Offa Rex* on one side and "There is no God but Allah" in Arabic, which would have been completely meaningless, there being not that many Arabic speakers in Dark Ages Anglo-Saxon England, except that they would have been vaguely aware that this was something a great empire stamped on its coins.

Fashion was influenced by France, then as now, and Offa was the first ruler to adopt fancy continental styles of dress, so much so that Alcuin complained of the king's love of fashionable Frankish clothes: "Some idiot thinks up a new-fangled idea and the next minute the whole country is trying to copy it."

More and more Anglo-Saxons were now travelling across western Europe although they still lived on the fringes of what remained of Latin civilisation. A sign of how isolated England was comes from the fact that in June 634 Pope Honorius sent a letter of address to Edwin and the Archbishop of Canterbury, unaware that the archbishop had been a fugitive for almost two years and Edwin dead for a similar length of time.

After England's conversion many Saxons went to "Saxony Overseas", as they called what is now Germany, to convert the people there, with whom they felt a strong affinity.[37] In 738 Boniface, who came from what is now Devon to go and preach on the continent, spoke of the continental Saxons being *de uno sanguine et de uno osse sumus*—"one and the same blood and bone", yet he was also aware of a distinct Anglo-Saxon identity, writing about "the race of the English" and himself as "a native of that same race". St Boniface became the patron saint of Germany after converting many people in that pagan land, although inevitably he was hacked to death by some angry heathens. These things never ended well.

The old Saxons, ancestors of today's Germans, were increasingly brought towards Christianity through evangelism. In the *Heliand* written in Old Saxon in the early ninth century, they were taught about Galileeland and Jerusalemburg, and how God lives in a great hall up in the sky. Even the Twelve Disciples are described as "warrior-companions", while the Last Supper is "final mead-hall feast".

While western Europe had suffered catastrophic population decline between the fourth and sixth centuries, it was around this period that it began to see an uptick in international trade, in particular focused on the Low Countries which even at this point seemed to be developing a nascent trading culture. There was also increasing activity among the Saxon trade emporiums, or *wic*, which had sprung up along sea lanes and rivers.

Among them were Lundenwic, which was described by Bede as "an emporium for many nations who come to it by land and sea". It was still tiny compared to Roman Londinium, and established a couple of miles to its west, something only fully confirmed in the 1980s when sixth-century rubbish pits were found under modern Covent Garden. Lundenwic was now under the control of Mercia's Offa, the most powerful king to date in English history.

Before he died, Offa had bullied the witan into accepting his son Ecgfrith as his heir, having him anointed as king in 787, in the Frankish style. Again, he was clearly influenced by Charlemagne, who had his own sons sent to Rome to emphasise his links with the old empire. This was the origin of the religious element of royal coronations that exists to the present day, and which had been adopted by all the barbarian kings hoping some Roman charisma would rub off; one of the great attractions of Christianity was that kings were able to draw on Roman culture and prestige.

Unfortunately, Ecgfrith died just a few weeks after the father's own passing and the line came to an end. Alcuin said it was the will of God while heavily hinting it was all Offa's fault: "For truly, as I think, that most noble young man has not died for his own sins; but the vengeance for the blood shed by the father had reached the son. For you know very well how much blood his father shed to secure the kingdom on his son. This was not a strengthening of his kingdom but its ruin." Alcuin never said this when Offa was alive, obviously; in fact he had written to the king calling him "the glory of Britain, the trumpet of the gospel, our sword and shield against the enemy".

By the end of his reign Offa was the most powerful Anglo-Saxon in history, and were his successors to have been as successful as him, the country's capital may have been somewhere in Staffordshire. Offa must have been remembered as a great king by many people. He was so well remembered that when Hertfordshire peasants rose up against serfdom in 1381 they cited the charters of King Offa as evidence that they were never to be unfree. That even the peasantry in this former part of Offa's kingdom still had an ancestral folk memory of his rule five centuries later testifies to the impact he had, even though they were woefully naïve about freedom in old Offa's reign; it's true they wouldn't have been serfs under his rule—they would have been slaves.

Western Europe's economy was recovering, boosted by growing literacy, trade, and relative peace. Indeed, an Anglo-Saxon scribe, possibly at the court of Alfred, coined a term to describe this new civilisation that had replaced the old—"Christendom". Yet this unchartered growth and progress was not to last, for as anyone who has ever moved up in the world knows, the worst nightmare imaginable is when uncouth, distant relations turn up and spoil things. And the Anglo-Saxons had the worst relatives imaginable—the Vikings.

CHAPTER 5

What the Vikings did for us

Vikings have historically got quite a bad press, being viewed in the popular imagination as a sort of ancient biker gang terrorising their way across northern Europe. On the other hand, recent historians have liked to focus on their commercial skills; as well as being heavily armed on their travels, they sometimes carried goods such as cloth for trade, no doubt marketed with the same emphasis on intimidation used by unemployed teenagers selling mops to an old age pensioner.

As well as this we should remember their nation-building in Russia and their achievements in sailing, famously reaching as far as North America. And they were certainly smart sailors: Raven Floki, known as Floki the Lucky, discovered Iceland by the clever trick of capturing three ravens and keeping them on board, then releasing them and following the birds, which can sense where the nearest land is.

Obviously, none of this revisionist history would have appeared as very reassuring to a Northumbrian monk who'd just had his monastery plundered and burned to the ground. Or to the poor souls who found their resting place at a Viking burial ground dating from 879, which contains two murdered slave girls beside a Viking warrior, as well as the jumbled remains of hundreds of men, women and children, just so the Norseman could torment their victims in Valhalla. Despite the modern trend for painting Vikings as just rather aggressive salesmen, the Scandinavian raiders were most definitely a terrifying menace, rightly compared to a plague by anyone unfortunate enough to have any contact with them.

No one called them Vikings at the time; that word simply means raider and only became common when the Icelandic sagas of the eleventh century were popularised in Victorian times.[38] To the Saxons they were sometimes called Danes, even if they were often Norwegian; both nationalities tended to rape and pillage, so it didn't really make much difference. More usually they were referred to as "heathens" or *pagani* (pagans).

Neither did they wear horned helmets in battle, as they are traditionally depicted in cartoons, an idea that mainly came about because of Richard Wagner's slightly sinister nineteenth century operas about the glories of the Nordic race in olden times.[39] The Vikings wore the same conical helmets as everyone else, although they did occasionally place horns or other ornaments on burial sites: in fact, most of the time they didn't wear any helmets.

The adventurous Greek mariner Pytheas may have visited Scandinavia in the fourth century BC during a trip where he first recorded and named the island that would become "Britain". He wrote of a further island called Thule where the people lived off wild berries because of a lack of crops and cattle, which may have been the Orkneys, Iceland, or Norway. The Romans called the area *Scadinavia*, which may mean "dangerous island", because the sea was dangerous, rather than the people. An N was later added in.

Although early Norse history is a mixture of hearsay, myth, and obviously made-up stuff, the earliest Swedish dynasty to create some sort of state was most likely a group called "the Ynglings". Being a Viking king was a tough job; one early ruler, Domaldi, was offered up by his own people as a human sacrifice to the gods after the crops failed in a moment of pure *Wicker Man* horror. Another Yngling king, Donnar, died "racked in pain in Sweden" although no further details are given. Then there was the strangely named king Eystein Fart, who died when a warlock he robbed, Skyjold of Varna, made a gust of wind rock his ship and he drowned.[40]

The original centre of ancient Scandinavian culture was most likely Old Uppsala, near modern-day Stockholm, and here archaeologists have discovered burial grounds of ancient kings, who were sent to

Valhalla with horses, dogs, and other animals, weaponry, grave goods and everyday objects, as well as rare treasures. Later writers say there were human sacrifices at this spot, which took place every nine years when nine males of various species—including men—were killed to please the gods.

Various Christian and Muslim writers described the Vikings as committing gruesome human sacrifices, with many of these horror stories coming in particular from Adam of Bremen, who was writing in 1072 after the Norsemen had been converted, and indeed after the Viking age had really ended. Many historians down the years have considered it Christian propaganda, perhaps in part because human sacrifice just seems too horrific, but modern forensics has shown it to be accurate, and clearly widespread, with several victims dug up across the Viking world, from Britain to Russia. A hill at Ballateare on the Isle of Man contains what may be the only human sacrifice known from Vikings in the British Isles, a female with a hole in her head.

Vikings perhaps believed that someone could take to Valhalla what they had buried in the ground and that's why they liked to bury a lot with them—including people. Not great for their slave victims, although handy for archaeologists. Human sacrifice was practised across the Viking world and the most famous account comes from Ibn Fadlan, a tenth-century Arab traveller who spent time with the Vikings in Russia, whom he affectionately called "Allah's filthiest creatures", in which he recalled how one young woman was sacrificed to accompany her master into the afterlife, after first having sex with all the men in the group, presumably after been drugged. It's easy to see how prudish Christians might have disapproved of all these shenanigans, which the ancestors of the Anglo-Saxons themselves practised according to one Roman writer.

At Uppsala the corpses of the human sacrifice victims were left on display even after Christianity had arrived in the region, and it is recorded that Christians had to pay a tax to avoid getting involved in the colourful local festival, which they were presumably happy to. But, as Christianity became more established, the practice had ended.

Norse religion was certainly quite cruel; the head of the gods was Odin to the Scandinavians, Woden or Wotan to Saxons further south, and he was especially worshipped by raiders. Odin was the god of battle and poetry, praised at banquets as a back-handed compliment to the host, and was known for his wisdom, but also his battle skills, riding on his eight-legged horse Sleipnir.

Among Odin's 200 names were Ghost-Lord, Ripper, Battle-Screamer, the Hawk, the Charging Rider, the Spear Lord, the Army Father, the Battle Blind, and the Author of Victory, which says something about the Viking culture—compare Jesus's titles, among them Prince of Peace, Lamb of God, the Good Shepherd etc. Indeed, of the names for Odin, some 25 per cent describe war and aggression and 11 per cent wisdom.

Odin was also called the Chooser of the Slain, the *valkojosandi*, and his female assistants were called *valkyrjur*; there were fifty-two of these Valkyries, among them Bright Battle, Ale-Rune, Taunts, War, Chaos, Devastation, Cruelty, Sword-Time, Killer, Unstable, Bossy, Shield-Scraper, Killer, Helmet-Clatter, Spear-Battle, Scent-of-Battle, and Teeth-Grinder. Valkyries were tragic female warriors, forever doomed to love mortal men in relationships that were obviously not ideal. Vikings believed that these otherworldly lovers of great warriors would protect them on the battlefield and, after they died, continue the relationship in the afterlife, and if they died in battle they went off to Valhalla (a Victorian misspelling of Valhöll). According to Viking folklore Odin and the Valkyries led wild hunts across the sky, seen as the *aurora borealis*, or Northern Lights.

In Norse myth Odin tried to avoid death at the battle of the end of the world by hanging upside down for nine days from Yggdrasil, a tree in deepest Scandinavia; for doing this he somehow received the forbidden knowledge of the runes which told him about the end of the world. Odin was portrayed sometimes as an old man ravaged by time, with a spear, a staff, and two ravens, the god usually one-eyed or occasionally blind. He is also called Jolnir, an elderly spirit of winter invited into people's homes during the midwinter festival of Yul; a sort of precursor to the central European Santa Claus, although somewhat less child-friendly and certainly not the kind of person you'd want visiting your house at Christmas these days. In Viking sagas Odin, like the other gods, interacted with people on earth; one Norse leader, Harald Wartooth, was visited by the god, who promised him invulnerability in return for the souls of the enemies he killed with his sword. Or so he claimed.

Odin was also patron of the men who stood at the front of battle, who wore no armour and were said to take on animal characteristics as they went into a frenzy; these warriors were known as wolf-skins and bear-shirts, *ulfhednar* and *berserkir*, from where we get the word "berserk". Although famed and feared, later sagas are less flattering of berserkers; one possible theory is that this is because earlier songs would have been sung with the minstrel in the same room as the berserker he was singing about, presumably glaring at him as he chose his words carefully.[41] There is also the theory that berserkers were largely propaganda stories designed to scare people and such frenzied behaviour would actually have been counterproductive, breaking up the lines; in Iceland acting like a berserker was banned during battle because it just got everyone killed.[42]

Then there is Freya, goddess of fertility and childbirth, and sometimes love, although she's an unusually violent goddess of love. Rather improbably, Freya goes into battle in a chariot drawn by two cats.

She's married to "Od" but takes many lovers, which apparently includes every elf in Asgard, and all the Aesir, the other family of gods, as well as a few dwarves and giants. She seduces kings and drives them to mutual destruction, and warriors who don't go to Valhalla might end up in Freya's *Sessrumnir*, or Seat-Room, which seemed to be equally prestigious.

But while those who fell in battle spent eternity in Valhalla, where they fought in the day and drank at night (anyone killed in the daytime would be brought back to life in time to join in the feasting), weaklings, mummy's boys, and bedwetters who died peacefully went to a very cold place called "Hel". All in all, Norse paganism looks like what you get if you let teenage boys design a religion, focused on fighting, fornication, and alcohol, whereas Christianity seemed to them like it was thought up by their mothers. The Vikings celebrated Yul, the midwinter festival, which involved drinking lots of ale and collecting cattle blood to turn into pudding, and which survives in our word Yuletide; it sounded like it was probably a bit more fun than the more sombre Christian midwinter festival, Christmas, although you were also probably more likely to end up being stabbed.

They were certainly not refined: they drank what they called *beor* but which tasted more like sweet fruity wine, and travellers from the Islamic world describe how they drank something so strong and disgusting that "people began to reel after a cup or two". Vikings would have ten-day funeral feasts, often dying from excessive drinking. To outsiders they must have looked quite terrifying, with archaeological finds suggesting that about one in ten men had their teeth carved to make them sharper and more scary.

Scandinavia was a society rich in fable and legend and strange creatures, as you might imagine of somewhere with months of long nights and high alcohol consumption. There were *alfar*, or elves, and their dark cousins, *dvergar*, dwarves. Bad dreams came from myths about malevolent creatures called *mares*, often associated with horses, from where we get nightmare. There were other beings such as *thyrs* (ogres) and trolls, too, while important places had guardian spirits, *landvoettir*. Viking shamans were often Finnish people, the Norsemens' eastern neighbours who they considered a bit strange. In the Norse mind inside us is a *hamingja*, which is almost like a physical impersonation of our luck. It also had its own will and might just walk off, which is why we still say "his luck ran out".

The Vikings' origin story is similarly fascinating and imaginative. They believed that the world began when the sparks from a great fire, the Muspelheim, began to melt the ice which had formed from a river of poison, the Elivagar. The droplets formed into a frost giant, Ymir, as well as a great hornless cow, Authumbla, whose milk sustained a race of giants. The cow licked the salt on the blocks of ice still formed in Ginnungagap, the frozen lake and this caused the first humans to be created. Meanwhile more giants emerged from the sweaty armpits of Ymir and then his legs mated with each other and produced a child, whose descendants would become a race of giants. Compared to the Christian origin story where God just made everything in six days, it seems incredibly complicated.

The frost giant Ymir dies and his body becomes the land, his blood the rivers and lakes, and even his teeth the rocks and bits of his brain the cloud. It's so heavy that four dwarves are sent out to the four corners of the earth to support the earth—Austri, Vestri, Nordri, and Sudri. Around this earth, the gods build a gate out of his remaining body parts—mainly eyelashes and eyebrows—which protects the world from the sea of blood which surrounds it. This wall is called Midgard, so that becomes the name of the earth where mortals dwell. To the east of this is Utgard, the home of demons, trolls, "and other horrors". To the north was Jotunheimr, Giant-Land or Giant-Lands. In Asgardr Gullinkambi the Golden Comb is a cockerel. Odin talks to the severed head of Mimr the sage and is told the future.

The Norsemen were perhaps unique in believing in an end time when everything would be destroyed—Ragnarök, a time of epic destruction, violence, and "whoredom", after which the universe will essentially end. It is believed that this legend grew out of the trauma of the sixth century and the great cooling caused by the volcanos of the 530s. Everything grew much colder, by as much as 4 degrees C, which caused immense misery across Europe but is obviously very bad news if you're already in Scandinavia. As many as half the population may have died in this cataclysm, and many scholars believe that much Norse myth reflects the trauma of this event. In one poem, Snorri's Edda, it is recalled a great winter will come, called Fimbulwinter, in which snow will come from all directions and "the sun will do no good", with three continuous winters.

Much of what we know about Norse society, recounted through later Icelandic Christian writers, originated with epic poems, which upper-class Norsemen would pay to have composed about their glorious adventures, or sometimes do it themselves. The *skelds*, or poets, were there to boast about the antics of their employers, so that their name will live forever, and possibly be the subject of dubiously accurate television shows a thousand years later.

Vikings tended to like strong and fearsome names, Bjorn (bear) and Ulf (wolf) both being common among Norse men, although they're better remembered for their epithets, among them Erik the Victorious, Bodvar the Wise, Eyjolf the Lame, Eyvind the Plagiarist, Halli the Sarcastic, Ivar Horse-Cock, Harold Wartooth, Wolf the Unwashed, and Thorkell the Skull-splitter. Women had colourful names too, like Thorkatla Bosom and Hallgerd Long-Legs.[43]

Far less flattering were the names given to the *thrall*, or slaves, the lowest of Scandinavian society's three social classes, below the *jarl* and *karl*. These slaves were given deliberately stupid names like Clot or Stinking for the men and Fat-thighs or Dumpy for the ladies, just as if their life wasn't terrible enough. Among the slave names in Scandinavian society were Fatty, Sluggisg, Bedmate, Badbreath, Greatgossip, Raggedyhips, Shouty, Bulgingcalves. The overall impression one gets of Viking society is one of hellish locker-room banter.

Having said that, being a slave in Scandinavia wasn't the worst thing in the world; you could be liberated if you were lucky, and the children of female slaves and free masters might also grow up free.[44] From thrall we get the word "enthralled", while jarl would become "earl" in English.

But for free men there was a certain equality. Viking raiders tended to share their booty equally, while the Norsemen held assemblies where they'd vote by brandishing their knives—"one man, one knife", you could call it. Their sense of comradeship was very strong, so much so that they went in for cutting their wrists and making themselves blood brothers.

And the Vikings did have some curious quirks. Norse women could divorce their husbands and keep their own surnames after marriage, and if they were together twenty years were entitled to half their possessions; overall they had far more power than women in any other society of the period, or for some time afterwards. To add to this progressive vibe, Scandinavian men were also known to wear bracelets and wash and look after their hair, and Norse haircuts became fashionable in Northumbria.

This is not to distract from the essential cruelty of their society, illustrated by the imaginative punishments meted out for wrongdoings. Men caught committing adultery with another man's wife could be trampled to death by a horse, those who killed their brothers were hanged by their heels next to a live wolf, while arsonists were burned at the stake.[45]

But perhaps what makes them so fascinating is their extraordinary adventurousness. Norse sailors reached as far as North America in the west and perhaps as far as the Persian Gulf in the east. On one occasion a group of sixty-two ships, setting out from the Loire River in central France, where they had encamped, raided distant Moorish Spain. They eventually sacked Morocco before one party headed back, arriving in Ireland where they were called the "blue men" by locals. Some Norsemen even managed to head all the way around Gibraltar and into the Mediterranean. In 859 two Viking leaders called Haesten and Bjorn Ironside planned on sacking Rome but Haesten, thinking he had reached the Eternal City, instead attacked the small town of Luna, 300 miles north; to be fair, to people who came from fishing villages ruled by people with names like Ivar Horse-cock, any Italian city would have looked pretty much like Rome.[46]

The Vikings and the Anglo-Saxons were closely related by ancestry and language, the latter having themselves only left Denmark 300 years previously. But while the Saxons had settled down and found God, the Vikings were aggressive, pagan, and suffering serious overcrowding at home—and as far as the Saxons were concerned these invaders in their 80ft longboats may as well have come straight from Hell; indeed, they were seen as punishment from God.

As Christianity had become established in England, and the economy had grown, monasteries like Lindisfarne had amassed a fair amount of wealth, since they were not subject to tax and monks did not have to join the army; in fact Bede said that many monasteries were in effect a tax scam where little prayer or anything constructive was done. Being "book-lands" they were free of royal demands, and so various people had even begun registering their homes as monasteries. As long as something was under Church control, it could expect to be spared the usual plunder and bloodshed between the warring kingdoms—but the Vikings obviously didn't play by these quaint rules.

A chronicler called Simeon of Durham wrote of the events of 793: "The pagans from the northern regions came with a naval force to Britain like stinging hornets and spread on all sides like fearful wolves, robbed, tore and slaughtered not only beasts of burden, sheep and oxen, but even priests and deacons, and companies of monks and nuns. And they came to the church of Lindisfarne, laid everything waste with grievous plundering, trampled the holy places with polluted steps, dug up the altars and seized all the treasures of the holy church. They killed some of the brothers, took some away with them in fetters, many they drove out, naked and loaded with insults, some they drowned in the sea."

The *Chronicle* reports that at the time of the raid there were immense whirlwinds and flashes of lightning, and fiery dragons seen flying in the air. This may have been a reference to Northern Lights, some historians believe, although the Anglo-Saxons loved this sort of end-of-the-world drama, fond of doomsday-like poetry about Armageddon. The tenth-century poem *Christ III* imagines the day when the stars are scattered, the moon falls from the sky, and the sun dies, leaving the world lit only by a bloodstained cross. It's quite a gloomy story, all in all.

Lindisfarne was obviously not the first raid, for the previous year Offa had imposed duties on churches in Kent for construction and repair of bridges and fortifications, and for expeditions *contra paganos marinos* (against heathen sailors). By 804 abbesses and abbots were beginning to locate monasteries away from the coast, with one Abbess Selethryth of Lyminge looking around Canterbury for a new home for a monastery, behind its city walls and away from the sea.

Despite the attacks many people still applied to join monasteries, whose members were also exempt from military service—not that this mattered to the raiders, for whom monasteries weren't exempt from plundering. The Vikings seemed to despise Christianity as a weak and feminine, and boring, religion; at worst they found it bizarre and amusing, while Christians feared and loathed Norse paganism.

Some historians now see the Viking raids as part of a wider religious war in the North, in which Christians were often the aggressors.

Charlemagne had put to death 5,000 Saxons who refused to convert to the new religion, and many pagan Germans, close relatives of the Anglo-Saxons, would have fled to Denmark with horrific tales of Christian oppression. It is certainly true that Christianity, once established institutionally, was usually merciless in crushing the old religion. Charlemagne's scholar Einhard wrote of the pagan Saxons that they "were a fierce people, given to the worship of devils, and hostile to our religion, and did not consider it dishonourable to transgress and violate all law, human and divine".

The pagans of the North perhaps saw an alien and intolerant religion on their doorstep pushing further into their homeland. Indeed, as far as back as 714 Anglo-Saxon missionaries had been trying to convert the Scandinavians, in the form of St Willibrord, who visited the Danish King Ongenus, a man described as "fiercer than any wild beast, and harder than stone". Willibrord spent forty years as a missionary in the country but had no luck.[47]

Yet while this may have been something of a holy war, many at the time attributed the attacks to divine anger. Alcuin, writing to King Ethelred of Northumbria, blamed the Viking raids on vice, corruption, "fornicating, adultery and incest" by nuns, short beards, luxurious clothes and even foxhunting by the clergy. Alcuin quoted the Book of Jeremiah: "Then the Lord said unto me, Out of the north an evil shall break forth on all inhabitants of the land." Alcuin, who often sounded like he was enjoying this doom-mongering, announced that "Behold, judgement has begun."

However, despite a widespread view that the heathens were agents of God's anger, the reason that these wild beasts began terrorising their neighbours was partly economic: the very north of Europe is poor in natural resources and during this period must have experienced huge population pressure—between the eighth and eleventh centuries 200,000 people left Scandinavia to settle elsewhere.[48] They didn't always make ideal immigrants, it's fair to say.

Viking society also probably had an extremely bad sex ratio because of polygamy, something outlawed by the Church, meaning that large numbers of young men had no hope of finding a partner at home. The poem of Helgi Hiovaardsson describes a king with four wives, which seems to have been not unusual, while the saga of King Harald Finehare describes how he "put away nine of his wives" as a condition of one marriage. There was also probably female infanticide, all of which further worsened the sex imbalance. Certainly, the tenth-century Normandy-based chronicler Dudo of Saint Quentin, living in a duchy founded by Vikings, suggested that the raids were the result of excess young men.

On top of this the development of new technology in shipbuilding allowed the Scandinavians to cross the North Sea in the eighth century, inside the famous vessels known as longships. These were typically about the length of a tennis court, and carried between thirty and sixty men.

The first known Viking raid took place off Saaremaa by Estonia in 750, the results of which were discovered between 2008 and 2012 with two boats full of dead Viking warriors buried there. The first had seven bodies, the second thirty-four, and while it was probably a raid some historians argue it was a diplomatic mission, although presumably not a very successful one if loads of people ended up dead.

The year 795 saw the first raid on Ireland, which was even easier to attack for the Norsemen because it was divided into hundreds of micro-kingdoms. The Scottish islands, perfect for the supreme seamen of the age, were also a target, and the Orkneys became the most heavily settled by the Vikings. Even the Picts, the famously terrifying tattooed maniacs of Caledonia who inspired the Romans to build a huge great wall to keep them out, suffered at the hands of Vikings; one excavation from Scotland revealed a charred building, smashed up sculptures and slashed-to-pieces corpses. There were occasional occupational hazards, however, to being a Viking. Sigurd the Powerful, first Norse earl of Orkney from 874, was killed in 890 after he had decapitated Pictish rival Mael Brigte the Bucktoothed in battle. Tragicomic mishap followed when Sigurd was riding around with Mael's head on his saddle, and his leg was scratched by the dead man's eponymously large tooth. Poor Sigurd died from the infection.

But the Vikings then went quiet for forty years in England. Perhaps one reason was that, a year after the Lindisfarne raid, they were delayed by bad weather at Jarrow during another excursion, and when they appeared at the riverbank the local men cut them to pieces, and sent the tortured corpse of their leader back to Scandinavia, which seems to have got the message across.

However, in 831, sixty ships appeared on the River Boyne in eastern Ireland and another sixty on the Liffey, and that same year between twenty-five and thirty-five ships landed at Carhampton in Somerset, right in the heart of Wessex. Saxon levies, farmers drafted in to fight, came from two counties but were beaten; the *Chronicle* records that the next serious raid was in 835 in Sheppey, Kent.

In 842 the Danes attacked London, burning down the bridge. Seven years later a huge fleet, said to be 350 ships strong, sacked Canterbury, and this time the invaders weren't just raiding and pillaging; they established a permanent home on Thanet in 850, the first time they wintered in England. Thanet, the same spot where the Jutes had first settled, was a strategically important spot for trading with the continent, and it was also home to nunneries, which tended to have plenty of gold. The Vikings then camped on the Seine for the winter of 852–853, for whenever things got a bit tricky in Britain, they just went off to Francia, and vice versa.

Francia was unfortunately at this point in the middle of a civil war between Charlemagne's grandsons, who were busy fighting over their inheritance just as Viking raids increased along the entire west coast, with a fleet of 100 attacking Paris in 845. The raiders were also active in the Low Counties and Aquitaine, which was so desolate after years of war and violence that chroniclers reported packs of wolves, 300-strong, roaming the countryside, devouring anyone they could. As for England, it was thinly populated, with almost no urban areas, no standing armies, and with much of it marked by wide waterways and marshes, so it was easy for seaborne raiders to cause havoc, and it was hard to resist a Viking war-band of thirty or so ships, called a *comitatus* by Latin-speaking chroniclers.

The raiders did sometimes lose battles, such as in 860 when the West Saxons "fought against the enemy, and putting them to flight, made themselves masters of the field of battle", according to Asser, and the Vikings "were cut down everywhere and, when they could resist no longer, they took to flight like women". However, generally speaking the Vikings won, because their armies were comprised of full-time warriors, while the Saxons were mostly farmers, even if major lords might have had their own small militias. In battle the Norse warriors used the bearded axe, the standard hooked axe one sees in medieval films, but also the Danish axe, which was larger and required two hands and was basically too unwieldy for all but the absurdly strong.

The Vikings were often happy to just indulge in blackmail and extortion rather than fighting. In 858 they captured the abbot of St-Denis near Paris and demanded a ransom so large that every church treasury nearby was drained. The *Codex Aureus*, a rich copy of the Gospels probably made in eighth-century Canterbury, has an inscription from an ealdorman (a local landowner and leader) called Alfred who explained how they had bought it back from Vikings for gold "because we did not want it to remain any longer in heathen hands". Such is the vast amount of silver extorted by the Vikings that on the island of Gotland alone 1,000 kilograms has been found, amounting to 168,000 coins.

A crisis turned into a national catastrophe in 865 with the arrival of the 3,000-strong Great Heathen Army, led by Halfdan, Ivarr, and Ubba, the three sons of the legendary Ragnar Lothbrok. Not much is known of these three men, except that Ivarr the Boneless may have had brittle bone disease, while Halfdan had the strange nickname "the Wide-embracer". Ragnar may have had another son, Bjorn Ironside, the legendary king of Sweden, if he existed.

Even less is definitely known about Ragnar, whose surname means "hairy trousers", acquired after he had worn special breeches to rescue his future wife from a monster. Ragnar appeared in many folk stories, and seemed to die in a variety ways, although the most famous is told in the *Tales of the Sons of Ragnar* where the hero is killed by King Aelle of Northumbria after being thrown in a snake pit.[49] *Ragnar's Saga*, as the Icelandic story is also called, says that he had only gone to England because he was jealous of his sons, and his untimely death there was apparently the cause of the invasion of England by the Danes, to avenge his death (although it's hardly like they needed a reason). No one is entirely sure if Ragnar even existed; a Ragnar attacked Paris in 845, but we don't know if it's the same as Lothbrok. That Ragnar apparently ended up suffering a terrible death back in Denmark, his stomach bursting open as his guts spilled out, so this would make a subsequent invasion of England difficult.[50]

It happened that the Viking invasion took place during a period of great instability in the four remaining English kingdoms; in this whole era just one Northumbrian king was peacefully succeeded by his son, while Mercia was being fought over by four different families, while also simultaneously at war with Wessex. The Great Army arrived en masse in East Anglia in 865, settling for the winter of 865–866, where according to the *Anglo-Saxon Chronicle* "they were provided with horses, and the East Anglians made peace with them". They then headed north and attacked the Northumbrian capital Eoforwic on November 1, 865, as the city was packed with people attending All Saints' Day Mass in its cathedral.

This was a common tactic used by the Vikings, who knew that Christians would not be prepared on religious festivals. The two bickering Northumbrian kings Aelle and Osberht were both there, but so busy arguing that they had not bothered to prepare for any attack, even though it was known the Vikings were nearby to the south. Aelle and Osberht both survived the assault, returning only once the Danes had left. However, in a subsequent attack on the Norsemen Osberht was killed, while Aelle was put to death by Ivarr and Halfdan using an especially cruel form of execution called the blood eagle, supposedly in revenge for killing their father. The blood eagle involved the victim's ribs being ripped out and then removed while he was still alive (it probably took some skill), after which his lungs were pulled out and spread across his back; he was then beheaded and chopped up.[51] It should be pointed out, and is by pedantic historians, that there is some doubt about this unusually cruel form of murder, which was only recounted three centuries later by Christian chroniclers. It is thought more likely that they just carved an eagle into his back, or had an eagle peck at him. At any rate he was dead by the end of it.

A puppet king called Egbert was installed, who after his predecessor's fate was understandably rather compliant, and the Vikings took control of the kingdom; unable to pronounce the name Eoforwic, they called it Jorvik, which eventually became York.

They then headed south, wintering in Nottingham in the English Midlands in 867, which back then—rather improbably—was called Snottingham. At this point a combined Mercian and West Saxon army approached the town but the Vikings did not join them in battle and the Mercians made peace. It was hard to keep any army in the field for too long, as the men had to return to their farms or their crops would rot. At some point the Mercian and West Saxon kings, Burgred and Ethelred of Wessex agreed for the first time that their kingdoms should have the silver penny as a common currency, a sign of how the Viking threat was pushing these two former enemies closer together—but it was to prove too late for the Mercians.

In 869 the Vikings returned to East Anglia and landed up in Thetford in Norfolk, at the time one of the largest settlements in England. The East Anglians resisted this time, not that it did them any good. Their King Edmund refused to renounce Christianity and became St Edmund after being shot to death with arrows. The *Anglo-Saxon Chronicle* says of Edmund merely that Ivarr "had the victory, and killed the king and conquered all the land" but a late tenth-century book called *The Passion of St Edmund* had the king demanding the Vikings convert, which rather fell on deaf ears, as they tied him to a tree and used him as target practice. According to another account Edmund waited in his hall, unarmed for Ivarr, and Ivarr had him beaten, whipped and speared, at which point he was apparently still alive. Then he was beheaded.

A legend also grew that his head was discarded but a grey wolf came to where it lay and said "Hic, hic" (here, here). Some people may be sceptical at this point, with a Latin-talking wolf entering the story, and perhaps more so when told that when the two parts of his body were finally collected the head miraculously reunited with the torso. His burial place became the site of Bury St Edmunds.[52]

The St Edmund martyrdom story seems heavily influenced by that of Sebastian, a popular third-century Roman saint who was shot to death with arrows and who often appears half nude and fashionably thin in highly homoerotic paintings that look like an early version of a Jean-Paul Gaultier advert. Overall, it's easy to see why people were not very positive about the Vikings. After their arrival monasteries at Ely, Peterborough, and Huntingdon were levelled, while the nuns at Collingham, just north of Berwick, cut off their own lips and noses to avoid being raped, and were killed instead.[53] Eighty monks were slaughtered at Peterborough cathedral in 870.

After the Danes conquered East Anglia, they followed it with the defeat of Mercia. Its last king, Burgred, went off to Rome on pilgrimage, which was quite common among rulers who were either unpopular or bored with their jobs but Burgred possibly didn't have much choice in his decision. Sadly, he died almost as soon as he reached the Eternal City. Burgred's wife Ethelswith fled to Wessex and then Rome but she didn't even make it that far, dying in Pavia. Again, a puppet was installed by the Vikings, a man called Ceowulf, dismissed by *The Anglo-Saxon Chronicle* as an "unwise king's thegn".

Northumbria, East Anglia, and now Mercia were all conquered, under the rule of the invaders. Only Wessex now remained, and at the end of 870 the Vikings arrived in Reading, inside the last kingdom.

CHAPTER 6

Wessex: the last kingdom

The kingdom of the West Saxons was traditionally founded by Cerdic, the leader who supposedly fought Arthur at Badon Hill, although Cerdic is a Celtic name and he may have been half British himself, if he existed.

Its most important king was probably Ine, who had come to the throne in 689, and who was possibly behind the creation of the Schola Saxonum, or Saxon School, a hostel for pilgrims in Rome, in an area of the city that was named after the English travellers who went there (although that could also have been Offa).

Most importantly, Ine also issued laws in 694, the first English codes outside Kent, which Alfred later cited, and also introduced the first coins in Wessex.[54] Ine ruled for such a long period, of thirty-five years, that he ended up abdicating to go to Rome on pilgrimage and stayed there.

Not a huge amount is known about earlier kings. There was a Sigeberht who was stabbed to death by a swineherd and replaced by Cynewulf, but he was then attacked by a Cyneheard—brother of Sigeberht—and the two men stabbed each other to death and so a man called Beorhtric was made king. After a while it all becomes rather confusing, and like the other Anglo-Saxon kingdoms, Wessex was racked by internal conflict. Alfred's grandfather Egbert, who became king in 802, had spent the previous sixteen years trying to seize the crown, spending much of it at the court of Charlemagne. There he had seen the steps taken by the emperor to stop raids by the Vikings, and after his rival Beorhtric died in 802 Egbert turned up and proclaimed himself king.

Beorhtric had been a sort of pawn of Mercia and made the mistake of marrying the great king Offa's daughter, the "grasping and wicked" Eadburh of Mercia (as Asser called her). According to the Welshman, "As soon as she had won the king's friendship and power throughout almost the entire kingdom, she began to behave like a tyrant after the manner of her father—to loathe every man whom Beorhtric liked, to do all things hateful to God and men, to denounce all those whom she could before the king." She also started poisoning people. Eventually Eadburh decided to do away with her husband's right-hand man because she didn't like him, either, but ended up accidentally killing her husband too.

Eadburh then fled to Charlemagne, king of the Franks, and he offered her the choice of marrying him or his son (presumably she hadn't told him an entirely truthful account of why her first marriage ended). She foolishly chose the son, to which the king replied that it was a trick question and "you will have neither him nor me", sending her off to a monastery. But even this didn't end well, and eventually she was caught in debauchery "with a man of her own race", ejected from the nunnery, and "shamefully spent her life in poverty and misery until her death" in Pavia, which was on the pilgrimage route to Rome and so familiar to quite a lot of English travellers.

As a result of Eadburh's behaviour the wives of the kings of Wessex were, uniquely in Europe, not styled queen, nor allowed to sit on the throne, which Asser calls "this perverse and detestable custom, contrary to the practice of all Germanic peoples". This is all the more perverse, as Wessex also had the only queen regnant known to have ruled any English kingdom before the time of the Tudors, Seaxburh, although she reigned only a year before her death in 674 and almost nothing is known of her.

Until the ninth century Wessex had been very much a lesser player on the scene, and its power rose just as Mercia descended into dynastic conflict, in particular in 821 when Mercia's king Coenwulf died and his son Cynehelm was murdered soon after by a jealous sister. Although early English history is made totally baffling by the sheer number of kings fighting each other, the family troubles in Mercia at this time are slightly easier to understand because everyone in one dynasty had a name beginning with C, and in another rival family they all began with B, another with W, and the last with L.

In 825, Wessex's Egbert beat Beornwulf of Mercia at the battle of Ellendum, in what is now Wiltshire, driving the Mercians across the Thames, and Egbert would go on to conquer Kent, Surrey, Sussex, and Essex. Even King Eanred of distant Northumbria paid tribute, after the king of Wessex led an expedition to the North. By 829 Egbert was so dominant that the *Chronicle* later described him as the eighth *bretwalda* and to celebrate his victory over rivals had coinage minted in Lundenwic, the Saxon settlement to the west of Roman London, which had previously been a Mercian city. The following year he had a pawn instated as an under-king in Mercia, around the same time as the Welsh also submitted to his rule. When Egbert died, in 839, he was succeeded by his son Ethelwulf without any drama; he was now totally triumphant and nothing, absolutely nothing could go wrong.

Ethelwulf is looked on by some historians as being a bit too holy and interested in religion rather than fighting, although the *Chronicle* records that he beat the Vikings at Aclea in Berkshire in 851 and there "made the greatest slaughter of a heathen that we have heard tell of up to the present day" (these reports do tend to get bogged down by superlatives, it should be noted).

Ethelwulf had a very religious circle of friends, some of whom would have an influence on his son, among them St Swithun, Bishop of Winchester, a man who, like Chad, was so humble that he would travel on foot rather than horseback; however, to avoid people thinking that this was false modesty he would only travel at night. Swithun, who died in 860, is behind the story that rain on his feast day would lead to a typical awful and wet English summer, a tradition that originated on Saturday July 15, 971, when the saint's body was moved by Bishop Ethelwold from the Old Minster at Winchester to a shrine inside. A storm blew up and it was taken as a sign of his unhappiness; after that it became a superstition that a wet July 15 would be followed by forty days of rain, which in England is often a good bet.

Ethelwulf and his wife Osburh had six children, who were called, with great originality, Æthelstan, Æthelswith, Æthelbald, Æethelberht, Æthelred, and Ælfred; "athel" means prince or throne-worthy, while the youngest child's name means literally "elf-counsel", elves being considered to be very wise creatures. The Æ, or "ash", was one of six now defunct letters in the old English alphabet, along with thorn (þ), wynn (ƿ), eth (ð), ethel (œ), and yogh (ȝ), but I've avoided using them because it's confusing enough listing people with various archaic names without adding more confusion with pretentious spelling.

Ethelswith, the only girl, married King Burgred of Mercia in 853 and like him had died in Italy. The three eldest boys were already fully grown warriors by the time of Ethelwulf's succession, while Ethelred and Alfred were perhaps a great deal younger. (History at this period is so vague that Athelstan may have been from a previous marriage of Ethelwulf, or he may have been his brother.)

The same year as the Vikings took Lundenwic, 849, Ethelwulf's youngest had been born some fifty miles west in Wantage, Berkshire.[55] According to Asser's slightly grovelling biography, Alfred's mother Osburh was "a most religious woman, noble in character and noble by birth. She was a daughter of Oslac, King Ethelwulf's famous butler," although butler might have been a more impressive job than it sounds to modern ears, and more like a chief minister. Oslac was supposedly descended from Goths and Jutes who were given the Isle of Wight by Cerdic, and who killed the last few Britons on the island at a place called "Wihtgarabyrig".

Since it wasn't expected that Alfred would ever be king, he was most likely given a more refined upbringing rather than the usual regal training, which mainly consisted of learning how to stab someone and guffawing loudly while eating a chicken wing (I'm perhaps being somewhat reductionist here). He was instead encouraged to take an interest in culture, although he possibly didn't fully learn to read until an adult. As a child of ten or so Alfred beat three older brothers in a competition set by his mother to memorise a book of poetry, at least according to his biography, which was written by someone in his pay. Although the young boy couldn't read, he got someone to recite it to him until he knew it by heart, and won the competition.

According to Asser's totally unbiased account, Alfred as a boy "surpassed all his brothers, both in wisdom and in all good habits. He was better looking, better behaved, a better huntsman and warrior." As a result, he was "greatly loved, more than all his brothers, by his mother and father—indeed, by everybody—with a universal and profound love".

Perhaps destined for the Church, he also took two pilgrimages to Rome as a child, a very hazardous route for a young person to go on; rather like taking your kids on holiday to Somalia or the Central African Republic today.

Rome certainly wasn't quite the great city it used to be. Rome had continued to shrink in the eighth century and when Alfred arrived it was home to perhaps 20,000 people, down from a million at its zenith. Although in contrast Wessex's capital of Winchester probably had fewer than 1,000 and Hamwic, the largest city in Wessex, "could have comfortably fitted inside the Baths of Caracalla in Rome", as one historian put it.[56]

The Catholic Church was also going through a troubled period, with numerous popes murdered during a period of intense backstabbing, even for Vatican standards. In one of the most bizarre episodes Pope Stephen VII had his predecessor Pope Formosus put on trial on charges of perjury and illegally becoming pope. The trial began in January 897 and Stephen was not remotely put off by the fact that the defendant was dead, and had his corpse brought to the courtroom where it was interrogated while sat in a chair.

"Why didst thou, tempted by ambition, dare to usurp the Apostolic See?" the defendant was asked by the prosecutor.

Silence greeted the courtroom, unsurprisingly really, as the defendant was dead.

The corpse was asked a number of questions but could not persuade the judge of its innocence and was found guilty. Strangely enough the episode rather reduced Pope Stephen's popularity, many of the faithful beginning to suspect he wasn't entirely mentally right for the job, and a few months later he was strangled to death. Popes certainly didn't need to resign back then; among the other pontiffs of the era, John VIII was poisoned and clubbed to death in 882, Leo V was strangled by a rival in 904, and John X died in a dungeon in 928.

Alfred's first trip took place when he was four, and it clearly made a big impression on the boy, who never forgot that Christianity was a link to Mediterranean civilisation and everything that came with it— philosophy, law, and most of all, literacy. According to his biography, Pope Leo IV anointed Alfred on this first trip, giving him a purple and white cloak and sword to signify he would be king, alongside the honorary title of consul; it's a nice story that suggests ruling was his destiny, but it's probably not true and rather the pope merely confirmed him into the faith, since Alfred had three older brothers so it looked very unlikely he would ever have been ruler. It's also suggested by historians that popes were quite generous with handing out these Roman trinkets and titles, which seemed to impress barbarian visitors, but probably weren't that much more significant than a "My dad went to Rome and all I got was this" T-shirt.

At some point in the next two years Alfred's mother died, and so aged six he took another trip to Rome in 856, this time with his father. Apparently Ethelwulf had begun his reign with two ambitions; one was to make the pilgrimage to Rome and see the relics. The second came from a vision, which he wrote about in a letter to the king the Franks.[57] In the letter, in which he asks for safe transit through Francia, Ethelwulf tells of a dream in which he is visited by a priest, who was himself visited in his dreams by a man who took him to an unknown kingdom with wonderful buildings. There they entered a beautiful church with boys reading books, and when they had a look at the books the priest found they were written in lines of alternative black ink and blood. When asked what this meant, he was told: "The lines of blood you can see in those books are all the various sins of Christian people, because they are so utterly unwilling to obey the orders and fulfil the precepts in those divine books. These boys now, moving about here and looking as if they are reading, are the souls of the saints who grieve every day over the sins and crimes of Christians and interceded for them so that they may finally be turned to repentance some day." So, to cut a long story short, he was going to France on holiday.

On the way back, they visited Francia, where the Frankish royal palace would have been daunting to the Saxon visitors, being hundreds of feet long, protected by round stone towers, walls carved with bas reliefs and huge statues, with marble mosaics and gilded furniture (at the time there were no two-storey buildings in England, except for Roman ruins).

Here Ethelwulf married a second time, to Judith of Francia, the daughter of its king, Charles the Bald (who wasn't actually bald, and no one knows why he got the nickname). Ethelwulf was somewhere between fifty and sixty, Judith was maybe thirteen or fourteen; it's safe to say it probably wasn't a love match. This was a period of increasing Viking activity, and historians have considered it a black mark against Ethelwulf's name that he decided to go off travelling, like a middle-aged man who leaves his wife to sort out the mortgage and childcare in order to "discover himself" in Thailand or Mexico. However, it's clear that the West Saxon king was trying to secure Frankish help against the Danes, and marriage alliances were the most effective way of doing so.

While Ethelwulf was overseas "a disgraceful episode" took place when his eldest surviving son Ethelbald, along with his bishop Ealhstan and ealdorman Eanwulf, conspired against the king. Together they tried to expel the old man from the land "but God did not allow it to happen, nor would the nobles of the whole of the Saxon land have any part it", as Asser reported. When he returned home Ethelwulf let Ethelbald keep the western half of the kingdom, which Asser describes as an "indescribable forbearance" on the part of the father towards his "iniquitous and grasping son".

Ethelwulf died in 858. A deeply religious man, his will stated that he "enjoined on his successors after him, right up to the final Day of Judgement, that for every ten hides [1200 acres] throughout all his hereditary land one poor man (whether native or foreigner) should be sustained with food, drink and clothing". Ethelwulf's will also included the stipulation that "300 mancuses", a measure of weight of gold, should be taken to Rome for the purchase of oil for lamps in the churches to be filled before Easter.

His eldest son Athelstan had been made king of Kent, which meant ruling a small part of Wessex in training for the big job, but he had died around 851; or at least, he's never mentioned again, so we can presume so. Ethelwulf was therefore replaced by the rather ungrateful Ethelbald in 858, and the new king soon shocked his family with his choice of wife. As Asser writes: "Once King Ethelwulf was dead, Ethelbald, his son, against God's prohibition and Christian dignity, and also contrary to the practice of all pagans, took over his father's marriage-bed and married Judith." To be fair, they were far closer in age than her previous husband (in fact the stepson was older) and she had come a long way for a mutually beneficial marriage alliance, and he was single, but for some reason everyone was disapproving.

The relationship didn't work out, since as well as being her stepson, Ethelbald was soon dead, having succumbed after only "two and a half lawless years", as his critic Asser called it. Judith went back home, and while waiting for her father to find her a new husband she eloped with Baldwin, count of Flanders and brother of Frankish king Louis the Stammerer (an understandably nervous man, who eventually got ill and died while on his way to fighting the Vikings). Eventually her father accepted her choice of husband and Judith and Baldwin lived happily ever after as far as could be possible at the time.

The next brother, Ethelbert, lasted a bit longer, dying in 865, from whatever ghastly malady took people away in the ninth century. He was probably lucky to, for that year the big Viking invasion was launched.

Alfred, meanwhile, had reached the age at which men were expected to become warriors, something which he proved to be competent at, although his real desire was learning, not fighting. Even by the standards of the age, Alfred seemed to be quite holy, right from an early age. He was tormented by his sexual desires, and according to Asser, when in "the first flowering of his youth ... and when he realised that he was unable to abstain from carnal desire, fearing that he would incur God's disfavour" he prayed that God would send him some mildly discomforting illness to keep his mind pure. After lots of prayer, "When he had done this frequently with great mental devotion, after some time he contracted the disease of piles [haemorrhoids] through God's gift." Thanks, God!

As he spent a lot of time on horseback it can't have been very pleasant. Alfred then prayed to God to take it away, and the haemorrhoids went; however, something much worse came soon enough. In 868, aged nineteen, he was married to a Mercian royal princess, Ealhswith, but on his wedding night, as Asser put it, "another more severe illness seized him" and Alfred was struck down by a severe pain. No one knew what this illness was, which lasted for twenty years, and according to Asser, "many, to be sure, alleged that it had happened through the spells and witchcraft of the people around him" or was the work of the devil or "the evil eye"; or, he speculates, it was "the piles" again. Some historians think it was Crohn's disease, an illness of the lining of the digestive system that causes a lot of pain in the bowels and stomach. It may also have been a psychosomatic or stress-induced illness, since he would get "savage attacks" whenever the Vikings attacked—and life was about to get a lot more stressful.

Tormented by his illness his whole life, Alfred eventually went to Cornwall and prayed to St Neot, a recently dead holy man from the area who was said to have been 4ft tall and who had renounced the worldly life to become a hermit. Alfred's malady was cured. Alfred was forty-five by this stage and had had the illness for all his adult life, and in fact he had just four or so years left to live. Still, better than nothing.

King Alfred

Her hiene bestæl se here on midne winter ofer tuelfan niht to Cippanhamme, 7 geridon Wesseaxna lond 7 gesæton [7] micel þæs folces [7] ofer sæ adræfdon, 7 þæs oþres þone mæstan dæl hie geridon, 7 him to gecirdon buton þam cyninge Ælfrede. 7 he lytle werede unieþelice æfter wudum for, 7 on morfæstenum.

"In this year the Host went secretly in midwinter after Twelfth night to Chippenham and rode over Wessex and occupied it, and drove a great part of the inhabitants overseas, and of the rest the greater part they reduced to submission, except Ælfred the king; and he with a small company moved under difficulties through woods and into inaccessible places in marshes."

The Vikings struck Wessex in 871, and the West Saxons met them that year at the Battle of Ashdown. Alfred was almost killed because his equally holy brother Ethelred was at prayer and so late to battle, although other accounts portray Alfred as reckless in starting early, fighting "like a boar". The battle was centred on a thorn tree with the two sides moving around it, pushing and jabbing at the enemy; the Saxons were victorious, five Viking earls were killed and Halfdan retreated to Reading. However, just a fortnight after, the Vikings won another battle, at Basing, and a few weeks later, King Ethelred died, on Easter Sunday, perhaps from wounds sustained in battle.

So it was that Alfred succeeded to the throne of Wessex on April 23, 871, and it would turn out to be a pretty stressful year, with nine battles, eight of which the Danes won. Strictly speaking Alfred had no great right to the throne, as Ethelred had two sons with a better claim; but in the Anglo-Saxon period there was no line of succession as such, only a pool of men considered throne-worthy, *athel*. Alfred had experience of battle and that's what mattered right now, although the people around him can't have been that hopeful by this stage. Things were looking very bleak for Wessex, and the Anglo-Saxons.

Alfred's reign started badly; a new Viking force had turned up, the Great Summer Army as it was called, and this combined with Halfdan's forces and defeated the Saxons at Wilton in Wiltshire. Alfred paid the Viking leader to leave him alone, a policy often used against pirates and which became popularly known as Danegeld later on; some of these coins used by Alfred to pay off the Danes turn up from time to time, with hoards found in such places as Croydon, Gravesend, and under Waterloo Bridge in central London.

In 873 the Vikings established a winter base at Repton in what is now Nottinghamshire, which had once been the Mercian royal mortuary as well as the site of a monastery, although it's believed that a lot of Vikings were buried there along with monks; of the 260 mostly male skeletons at the site, 45 per cent have blade wounds to the head. The corpses were placed around a giant, who was apparently 9ft according to the agricultural labourer who discovered it in 1686, before the skeleton was lost.[58] He may have been lying.

Repton is also the last resting place of the Repton Warrior, a corpse that gives us some clue to old-fashioned Viking ideas of masculinity. The warrior, an unknown man aged between thirty-five and forty-five, had had his genitals cut off after death, quite a common feature of medieval battle where the losers were often mutilated in fits of rage. The Vikings buried him with a boar's tusk between his legs, presumably because they wanted him to have a penis in the eternal bachelor party that is Valhalla. The Repton Warrior may even be Ivarr the Boneless, who seems to have died horribly at around this point. Repton is also the last resting place of some victims of human sacrifice, and an added curiosity is that 20 per cent of the Viking warriors buried here are female, which lends currency to the idea that there may in fact have been the type of badass Viking girlbosses who television and film producers are so keen on.

By 874 the Vikings had fully established their rule over three of the Anglo-Saxon kingdoms, which would have made it easier to put pressure on what was left of the last kingdom; the following year the Vikings began settling the land, parcelling out swathes of the North and Midlands to supporters, establishing farms and bringing over women. It might well have looked like the Danes would overrun the Saxons and make England theirs.

That same year, 875, a Viking warlord called Guthrum mustered an army at Cambridge for another assault on Wessex. However, when he crossed the frontier, he was besieged by a West Saxon army, and they only let him go on condition he promised not to invade again. Obviously, he didn't keep this promise, despite swearing on the pagan gods, and sailed around to Exeter, waiting for a Danish fleet to land.

Alfred made peace with the Vikings at Wareham in Dorset in 876 but, according to Asser, "practising their usual treachery … And paying no heed to the hostages, the oath and the promise of faith, they broke the treaty," and Guthrum killed all the Saxon hostages Alfred had handed over. To the pagans, Christian ideas of the rules of war were meaningless, and oaths made to the Christians empty words. In contrast Christian leaders seemed to continually demand that Vikings swore oaths or took baptism, even though they repeatedly went back on their word, in the vague hope that one day they'd see the light. Yet there did seem to be some divine justice. The Vikings now landed in Exeter, where they were blown away in a storm, with as many as 120 ships destroyed, and the loss of 3,600 men. (Again, a caveat about figures—that seems like an awful lot of people.)

Despite this brief interlude from the relentless bad news, by the end of 877 the situation was desperate for Alfred; the Danes held Exeter and Gloucester, deep inside Wessex, and now refused to leave at all, with or without money. On Twelfth Night, January 6, 878, the invaders launched an attack on Chippenham, where what was left of the royal court had been celebrating Christmas, killing almost everyone. The last English king barely escaped with his life, slipping away before Guthrum could find him. He was trapped and surrounded, a fugitive. Alfred fled into the wilderness, to the Isle of Athelney, the last refuge of the Anglo-Saxons.

Much of England is naturally marshland, including large areas of the East Midlands and South-West, and during the ninth century this part of Somerset was either under water or marshy. Here Alfred and his small band of followers now held out; it was Alfred's lowest point, and although still under thirty he was in poor health and broken by the sheer awfulness of life. The odds were now overwhelmingly against him, against Wessex, and against England.

This is the period of the most famous story attached to the king: anonymously wandering through the woods, he came to a poor couple's house and was allowed to rest there for a couple of nights, after some persuasion. At some point he was sitting by the fire and the woman of the house asked if he would watch the bread (or cakes) as it cooked. The woman had no idea who he was and assumed he was just some random farmhand her husband had taken pity on or brought in to do odd jobs. Alfred, with his mind understandably on other matters, let the bread burn, and so the poor woman scolded him.

The story tells an important moral about the man: Alfred was such a good chap that he accepted the woman's telling him off rather than pointing out that he had more important things to worry about than her bread, such as beating the Vikings. The tale first appeared in the tenth-century biography of tiny saint St Neot, soon enough after the event to suggest some plausibility, and what's more, it's the only detailed account of the king that didn't arise from his own PR machine, but sadly no historian considers it to be true. (Another, much later, and even less plausible story has him walking into the Viking camp disguised as a travelling minstrel—about as likely as the American president strolling around a Middle Eastern capital with a headscarf, *Team America*-style.)

At any rate Alfred and the cakes became a popular tale, appearing in Victorian history books with illustrations showing the serious-minded

Englishman trying to concentrate on important worldly matters of state while the woman in the corner blathers away about nothing of importance.

During his darkest moments it was also said that dead saints visited Alfred, among them St Swithun, whom he would have known as a child. Another story has a poor man turning up and asking for some food; despite his own dreadful poverty, Alfred gives him half of what little he has, only for the beggar to reveal himself as none other than seventh-century celebrity saint, Cuthbert of Lindisfarne.

The holy man then repays his generosity by inspiring a miraculous haul of fishes for Alfred's men, and then giving the king some tactical advice, and telling him that "All Albion is given to you and your sons."

Sceptics might not totally believe that one, but Alfred's attachment to Cuthbert, the most important of the Northumbrian saints, is significant. Already Cuthbert was so revered that it was believed that anyone who failed to treat his memory with reverence was plagued with madness and "a loathsome stench",[59] and even the Vikings were wary of desecrating his shrine in Northumbria. But he was also a northern saint, and Alfred's devotion reflected a desire to claim all of the Anglo-Saxons' heritage as his own. He would not just save Wessex, but all of England.

Alfred now had a stroke of luck. Early in 878, while the king was trapped by Guthrum and his men, a group of Saxons under an ealdorman in Devon called Odda were besieged at Countisbury Hill by the terrifying-sounding Viking maniac Ubba (or alternatively, Hubba). Ubba, one of the three sons of Ragnar, had landed at Lynmouth and saw ealdorman Odda and his men waiting. The West Saxons were mostly farmers and peasants, armed with whatever agricultural implements they could get their hands on, and must have been scared witless at the prospect of what they faced. Before battle, Ubba would have flown the raven banner "sacred to Odin, Gallows Lord and All-Father" in battle; it had been woven by his sisters and it was believed it would fly strong before victory but hang limp before an impending defeat, presumably accompanied by a sort of Benny Hill impotence sound effect. The omens were good that day for Ubba—the banner flew. Expecting the Saxons to stay put in expectation of relief, the Danes surrounded them and waited for the English to starve, so were surprised when Odda and his men suddenly stormed down the hill, killing up to 1,200 Danes, including Ubba (usual number caveats apply).

And then came Alfred's great Hollywood moment. It was the custom in Anglo-Saxon society that all free men were obliged to bear arms for their lord when required, fighting in the *fyrd*, the traditional Anglo-Saxon militia. The *fyrd* dated back to the very earliest Saxon kingdoms, and even after the Norman Conquest the system survived to a large extent.

Over the winter the king had sent his followers around what was left of Wessex to spread the word that all men were to meet at Egbert's Stone in Wiltshire between May 4 and 10, 878, the seventh week after Easter. And so, after months of hiding and isolation and strange visits from dead holy men and being told off by women, Alfred arrived at the spot and saw that the men of Somerset, Wiltshire, and Hampshire had arrived—thousands of them. According to Asser: "When they saw the king, receiving him (not surprisingly) as if one restored to life after suffering such great tribulations, they were filled with immense joy." Cue John Williams soundtrack, and one presumes, a stirring speech by the king.

The crucial fight came on May 12, 878 at Ethandum, an event now known as the Battle of Edington because that's the village where most people think it was. Battle in the early medieval period consisted of two lines of men facing each other, close together in tight formation, protected by a row of shields and desperately trying to stab whatever they could through the holes in the shield wall; behind the front line would have been another row of men giving support and protecting the flank, like a scrum in a really, really scary game of rugby in which the opposition were trying to knife you in the face. The battle would have been preceded by the drumming of swords on shields, as the men psyched themselves up for the fight; then would come the javelins, followed by the charge.

Asser reports in the *Life of Alfred* that at Edington the Saxons were "fighting ferociously, forming a dense shield-wall against the whole army of the Pagans, and striving long and bravely … at last he [Alfred] gained the victory. He overthrew the Pagans with great slaughter, and smiting the fugitives, he pursued them as far as the fortress."

Unfortunately, this being the early Middle Ages, almost nothing else is known of what actually happened, except that a lot of people met very gruesome ends. In many if not most battles of the period we don't even know where the fight took place, so that for the most important battle in English history before 1066, the Battle of Brunanburh, in 937, which led to the unification of England, there are forty different possible locations, anywhere from Merseyside to the Scottish borders. Edington has been located in four different counties.

The battle ended with the surviving Danes surrounded on a hilltop, where after two weeks the starving remnants surrendered. In the treaty that followed Guthrum was forced to hand over a number of hostages, who might well have expected to be killed, since that's what Guthrum would have done, but the king was merciful. "When he had heard their embassy, the king (as is his wont) was moved to compassion and took as many chosen hostages from them as he wanted," Asser said. His Christian faith was at the heart of everything Alfred did, and he really lived up to it.

Under the terms of the treaty the Danes would keep East Anglia, Northumbria, and the eastern part of Mercia, recognising Alfred's rule in Wessex and the western part of the middle kingdom. England was therefore split in two, and the Anglo-Saxons, having looked like they were doomed, now controlled everything west of Watling Street, the old Roman road that went from London up to north Wales. In the treaty with Guthrum, it was declared that King Alfred acted with "all the counsellors of the English race", the *Angelcynnes witan.* He was now undisputed leader of the English.

Guthrum also agreed to baptism, with Alfred as the odd choice of godfather (unlikely to receive any birthday cards), but this wasn't just because Alfred forced him; to Guthrum's way of thinking Alfred's victory was proof that this Christian God might not be a weakling after all, and could even help him win battles if they maybe went easy on the "blood eagle" shenanigans. The baptism party lasted twelve days, and the English celebrated by drawing another chalk white horse. Guthrum was now Athelstan, his baptismal name.

Alfred had some respite, and would use it wisely. As it turned out in 885 Guthrum tried invading again—he just couldn't help himself—but he was easily defeated this time. The reason was that in the meantime Alfred had been busy, using his great interest in learning to create for the first time the infrastructure of a state.

CHAPTER 7

The life of Alfred

Had the last of Ethelwulf's sons just beaten back the Vikings, that would have been impressive enough, but he also had higher aspirations for the country, and a vision of civilisation. King Alfred established the first national law codes, created an education system, founded a navy, built a network of cities and set up a national chronicle that would record events from across the country.

Most of what we know about Alfred comes from Asser, who came from a monastery at St David's in Wales and first visited the king in Sussex some time in 886. How they came to know each other is a mystery but Alfred was obviously impressed and offered him a job; Asser took it on agreement that he could work in England for six months a year and spend the rest in Wales. However, on the way back from Sussex to ask permission from his abbot he fell ill with a fever and spent a year in Winchester recovering. Eventually he consulted his fellow monks, and Asser's people accepted the offer so long as Alfred helped the Britons in one of their interminable internecine wars, in this case against someone called King Hyfaidd. Asser took the job in 887: that same year Alfred learned Latin.

The Life was written after Asser retired, and perhaps for a Welsh audience, something we can guess at it because in it he explains the

Welsh names for English towns such as Nottingham (Tig Guocobauc). Asser introduces his subject as "Alfred, ruler of all the Christians of the island of Britain, king of the Angles and Saxons" and himself as "Asser, lowest of all the servants of God" who wishes his king "thousand-fold prosperity". Clearly, it's not a hugely critical biography, and that sort of remains the tone throughout. The book ends abruptly, which suggests that either bits of it were lost or Asser died while writing it; or maybe he just gave up and lost heart, thinking no one would be interested in a boring story of how a king beat the Vikings.

Asser was sort of Alfred's PR man and was rewarded handsomely, among his benefits being "an extremely valuable silk cloak and a quantity of incense weighing as much as a stout man".[60] (The definition of a fat man was probably different then.) Alfred would get Asser to read to him, until in his twenties he learned to read and later taught himself Latin. Before his reforms Alfred complained that not a single man living south of the Thames could understand the language of the Church, so he took the lead by learning it—by this stage he was in his forties, which was old age at the time.

King Alfred, like many Englishmen through the ages, felt that the country had gone downhill, and he looked back at the seventh century as the golden age when kings "not only maintained their peace, morality and authority at home but also extended their territory outside". He may have exaggerated just how good that century really was, but it's true that, with the Vikings having destroyed pretty much every monastery they could find, there had been a decline in literacy as a result, monasteries being where most of the books and most of the literate people were based.

Alfred's literacy drive was perhaps almost as impressive as his battles against the Vikings, although admittedly not quite so easy to set to epic music. He built schools and re-founded earlier places of learning that had been left derelict; he also made local councillors read so that everything could be kept in order; and he established a court school, as the Franks had, to educate the nobility.

Alfred personally translated from Latin to English a number of the most important books he thought it necessary for civilised people to understand; his first effort, which was called simply "the handbook", contained translations of various Latin works, but unfortunately it has since been lost. Among the major texts he turned into English are Bede's *Ecclesiastical History*; Pope Gregory's *Dialogues* and *Pastoral Care*, a copy of which has "Alfred translated me" in the preface; and Paulus

Orosius's *Histories against the Pagans*, a fifth-century work by a Spanish priest which sought to counter the argument that Rome's decline was due to Christianity (a sort of prototype to the modern polemic which proves how all the reader's political prejudices are correct).

Perhaps the most significant of Alfred's translations was *The Consolation of Philosophy* by Boethius, a sixth-century lament considered the last great work of antiquity, in which the philosopher reflects on why God allows terrible things to happen and how we should find happiness among the misery. Boethius was a Roman who found himself in prison at the hands of the Goths over some pedantic theological issue, and was eventually executed for it; compared to him, Alfred's life was like that of a Regency dandy.

It is even believed that Alfred provided his own epitaph in this passage which he translated from Boethius: "I desired to live worthily as long as I lived, and to leave after my life, to the men who should come after me, the memory of me in good works."

Alfred also recruited a number of people from the Continent to aid learning, summoning "certain luminaries" from across Britain to join them. He established two monasteries, one at Athelney, and hired "John the Old Saxon" (that is, from "Old" Saxony in Germany) in 885 to be the abbot there. John the Old Saxon may have taught Alfred as a youngster and had a reputation as something of a disciplinarian, and for whatever reason John didn't get on with the priest and deacon there, who were both from Gaul. They, with the help of two Gallic slaves, hatched a plan to kill him on his way home from church, the idea being to murder the abbot by the altar and dump the body outside the house of a prostitute, so making it look like he was killed in some squalid and embarrassing vice-related dispute.

A cunning plan—however, in a dramatic twist straight from a 1980s action film, it turned out that John, in the words of Asser, was "a man of customary sharp intelligence … and a man with some experience in the martial arts". Although badly wounded, the Old Saxon survived and was able to inform the authorities, and after an investigation all four assailants "underwent a terrible death through various tortures". Another abbot, called John the Scot, was brought over from France in 877, and was stabbed to death by his own pupils with their metal pens.[61] A more challenging age.

Alfred remained obsessed with learning throughout his life, and as Asser wrote: "By day or night, whenever he had any opportunity, he used to tell them to read aloud from books in his presence—indeed he could never tolerate being without one or other of them—and accordingly he acquired some acquaintance with almost all books, even though he could not at this point understand anything in the books." Alfred also made all his ealdormen learn to read or else "to relinquish immediately the offices of worldly power that you possess".

Perhaps his greatest achievement was starting the *Anglo-Saxon Chronicle*, a record of events updated annually at five locations around the country, written in the native language so everyone could understand them. The *Chronicle* also charts known history back to the time of Christ and records events in Britain since the arrival of Hengest and Horsa and the Anglo-Saxons. It records all that was known of the most obscure years, a typical entry being that of 682: "this year Centwine chased the Britons into the sea". (Centwine was king of Wessex and that line is all we know of his life, except that he eventually abdicated to become a monk.) No other country in the world had anything vaguely resembling the *Chronicle*, which would last until the mid-twelfth century, written by that stage with increasing sarcasm about the new Norman rulers.

It contains not just a record of events but also the oldest piece of English prose, telling the story of how King Cynewulf of Wessex is set upon while visiting his mistress in 757, a piece of prose which we know to be older than the *Chronicle* in which it features because the structure is more archaic.

The bulk of the *Chronicle* dealt in misery, a tone the entries maintain for two and a half centuries, with cheery events such as these:

> 851 Ealdorman Ceorl, with the men of Devon, fought with heathen men ... made great slaughter and took the victory ... They (the Danes) ruined Canterbury, put to flight Beorhtwulf the Mercian king and his troops.
>
> 870 The Danes killed the king (St Edmund) and overcame all the land. They destroyed all the churches they came to.
>
> 874 They (the Danes) drove the king, Burgred, over the sea; and they overcame all the land.

Without the *Chronicle* and Alfred's other literacy efforts our knowledge of the period would be staggeringly thin.

Western European monarchs were still picking up the pieces of what Roman civilisation had left and the best way of recapturing the glories of

Rome was through the Church. So Alfred made a habit of sending regular embassies to Rome, and in return in 882 Pope Marinus sent Alfred a piece of the True Cross that Jesus died on (one of the more dubious genre of relics of the medieval period—there was by one estimate enough of the True Cross going around to build three ships at one point).

Although England was increasingly drawn into a wider Catholic cultural world stretching from the North Sea to Italy, Alfred was also the first king to have a world vision; he not only made an alliance with the Franks against the Vikings, although the Franks went back on their word and let the Vikings camp on their land; he also sent money to the Christian mission in India; the king even became a sort of pen pal with the ruler of Jerusalem.[62]

Alfred, once he had raised enough money, divided the royal revenue in three. The first part went to fighting men "and noble thegn", that is, the aristocracy. "The second portion he gave to his craftsmen, who were skilled in every earthly craft." And Asser adds that "with a cheerful disposition, he paid out the third portion to foreigners of all races who came to him from places near and far and asked money from him (or even if they did not), to each according to his particular station". This sounds like the sort of policy that wouldn't be very popular today—"let's just hand out money to any random foreigner who turns up"—but Viking-ravaged ninth-century England wasn't a huge destination for travellers or benefit tourists.

In 891, for instance, the *Chronicle* records that "three Irishmen came to King Alfred in a boat without any oars from Ireland, whence they had stolen away because they wished to go on pilgrimage for love of God and cared not where. The boat in which they travelled was made from two and a half hides." Despite this almost comical recklessness they made it across the sea and were able to entertain Alfred's court with their tales, and at the time this would be literally the most exciting thing that would happen at court for years.

Eventually the holy Irishmen departed on their mission to reach Jerusalem, and no one knows what happened to them; something awful, probably. On another occasion a Norwegian called Ohthere or Ottar visited Alfred's court. He came from near Tromsø, or as he told Alfred, "the farthest north of all Norwegians". Ottar was very rich as he possessed over 600 reindeer and some other animals, and told the court how he received tributes from the Saami people, reindeer herders who lived in the north of Scandinavia. He explained how he had travelled up the coast of Norway for four days until the coastline turned south, so reaching the most northerly point of mainland Europe; he then sailed for a further five days and there he met some Finnish peoples.[63] These weren't the only visitors—Alfred's court would come to be multinational for its day, including "many Franks, Frisians, Gauls, pagan Danes, Welsh, Scots and Britons".[64]

The king also laid down the first national English legal system, a mixture of old Anglo-Saxon customs and biblical commandments, the "Doom book" as it was called, doom meaning "law". He begins it, naturally, with a preamble explaining his thoughts on the Bible—Alfred never missed a chance to shoehorn in religion—and although in legal terms the code is contradictory in places, it is all based around a philosophy of Christian kingship. In his laws Alfred cited previous kings such as Ethelbert of Kent, Offa, and Ine, in doing so claiming the inheritance of all the Anglo-Saxons.

He declared that no Englishman, however poor, should be outside the law: "Doom very evenly! Do not doom one doom to the rich; another to the poor! Nor doom one doom to your friend; another to your foe." This would be a fundamental principle of English common law down the ages, as adopted in the United States and other colonies (even if in practice it's not always observed).

In reality, the Anglo-Saxons had a system of justice that valued the lives of poor men less than rich; under their legal system *wergild* ("man money") was the value of a man's life, the amount his family had to be compensated if he was killed or injured, depending on social status (the Anglo-Saxon word for man still survives in *werewolf*). Under the wergild system the king was valued at 120 pounds, the same as six thegns or thirty-six peasants, while the Britons, or *Welsh*, were worth half the equivalent status of a Saxon. It was a legacy of the archaic system of justice being meted out by blood vengeance, so that if someone killed your brother, you killed them, after which their brother killed you, and so on and so on for years and decades. In some ways status was more important than social class: a man who was "oath-worthy" could give evidence in court, and to lose this status was devastating.

Since there were no jails, most crime that didn't involve execution consisted of fines or maiming; so that under Alfred's law, fondling the breast of a freewoman brought you a five shilling fine, leading to ten shillings for sexual assault and sixty shillings for rape. Other blood money payments seem a bit bizarre: it was sixty shillings for a lost nose in a fight, twenty shillings for a big toe, down to one shilling for the nail of the little finger. But if your dog killed someone, you'd only have to pay a six shilling fine (rising to twelve shillings for the second killing and thirty shillings for the third—after which it must have got a tiny bit suspicious). And while if you accidentally killed a man by felling a tree, you only had to give his family the tree as compensation, which hardly seems a reasonable exchange; the fine for accidentally stabbing a man depended on the angle of the wound, which suggested how "accidental" it was.

During this period men were divided up into tithings, groups of ten men who were responsible for each other's behaviour, so that if one broke the law the others had to bring him to justice; they in turn grouped into groups of 100, who were responsible for chasing fugitives, in what later became called the *posse comitatus* (and so a "posse" in westerns). They would dispense justice and once a month would get together and drink lots of beer, so as one historian noted: "Anglo-Saxons at the highest level were accustomed to take decisions of the most serious import at drinking sessions, the frequency of which helps explain why this was such a violent society."[65] The combination of justice and alcohol is always a sensible idea.

The Anglo-Saxons drank "oceanic" amounts of beer, as one historian put it, and even local government entirely revolved around beer-drinking sessions, with each parish having a guildhouse (a drinking house) where decisions were made. The communal meeting was known as "an assembly of drinkers".[66] St Boniface, having travelled across much of Europe, was perhaps the first to observe a particular national character trait, complaining that among his people "the vice of drunkenness is too frequent. This is an evil peculiar to pagans and to our race. Neither the Franks nor the Gauls nor the Lombards nor the Romans nor the Greeks commit it."

Although Alfred played a huge part in the creation of a justice system, it can be exaggerated. Later in the medieval period, when lots of things became associated with Alfred that weren't really anything to do with him, he was seen as inventing that quintessential part of English justice, the jury system; while something resembling it may have been around by AD 1000, it wasn't until the reign of Henry II (1154–1189) that juries were established.

Among his other reforms, however, Alfred did standardise the currency of Wessex and Mercia, and improved its quality; silver content went up from 0 to 20 per cent. It's one thing to win battles, of course, but Alfred was also good at the boring and necessary elements of administration. In order to increase and improve the ranks of the nobility, which was now thin on the ground, he decreed that anyone who had 400 acres of land might become a thegn; likewise, any merchant could officially join the upper class if he could show he had travelled abroad three times at his own expense.[67]

Alfred is also supposed to have invented a sort of clock. This came about after he said he would devote eight hours a day to God, eight hours to public business, and eight hours to rest and recreation, a fairly gruelling schedule that didn't leave much "me" time. Because sundials were a bit shaky as a form of measuring time, he worked out that a candle of twelve pennyweights of wax burned exactly four hours, and made his chaplains, among them the rather unfortunately named Werewulf of Mercia, find him seventy-two pennyweights of wax, so six candles could be burned for twenty-four hours. He ordered clergy to keep track of time, and also built lanterns to protect them from the wind (there were no glass windows at the time).

As Asser said of him: "Just like the clever bee which at first light in summertime departs from its beloved honeycomb, finds its way with swift flight on its unpredictable journey through the air, lights upon the many and various flowers of grasses, plants and shrubs, discovers what pleases it most and then carries it back home, King Alfred directed the eyes of his mind far afield and sought without what he did not possess within, that is to say, within his own kingdom."

Another impressive legacy was the Alfred Jewel, a two and a half inch long broach made of gold and quartz which has "Alfred made me" written on it. It was discovered in 1693 on farmland in Somerset, and now rests in the Ashmolean Museum in Oxford; scholars have debated for centuries what it actually is, but they now seem to agree it was used for pointing at text while reading.

Even if some of his achievements were exaggerated, Alfred achieved huge amounts in his reign; he was a man way ahead of his time, who must have been frustrated by the idiocy around him. Indeed, Asser complains that Alfred had to contend with the people's "common foolishness and obstinacy", lamenting "I could mention fortifications ordered by him but not yet begun, or begun too late to be finished."

Alfred achieved all this despite being something of a neurotic and hypochondriac, obsessed throughout his life with the idea that he was coming down with a horrible disease or going mad; this may have been related to the torment he felt about his own sexual desires, which he considered sinful. He was constantly anxious about everything, so as his biographer said of him: "What shall I say of his daily concern for the people who live from the Tyrrhenian Sea to the far side of Ireland." As if he didn't have enough problems on his plate without worrying about the Balkans.

The Danes attack again, inevitably

The king, just as importantly, made military reforms, among his innovations being the creation of "burhs", or boroughs, cities that were also fortresses. Here large numbers of civilians congregated for security, and in this he was almost certainly influenced by the Franks, who had begun to do something similar.

The idea was that no one would be more than fifteen miles from refuge, and it led to the foundation of many towns of importance, among them Warwick, Worcester, Chichester, and Hastings. Some of the burhs were former Roman settlements rebuilt, while others were new altogether. A document surviving from this era, the Burghal Hidage, recalls that each town was responsible for being able to feed a certain number of men who could man its wall, depending on its size, with each recruit expected to defend just over four feet of wall.

So long as everyone could get to a burh in time they would be safe until the king's army arrived, since the Vikings were not very good at siege warfare, as they tended to get bored easily. The roads King Alfred built to link these towns—the *herepaths*—were also an important part of his kingdom's growing infrastructure. Alfred also built up his capital of Winchester, turning it into something approximating a city, with six miles of cobbled roads, channels alongside each street to supply drinking water to its growing population, and a market.

It was no longer enough to simply have a militia turning up after the Vikings had arrived and killed everyone; under Alfred's reforms the king's followers were divided into three shifts, so that one third were always at the royal court ready to fight while the rest were farming; were the Vikings to attack again, he would be able to call on thousands of men. And inevitably they would attack again.

Outside Wessex, there remained some resistance to foreign rule. In Northumbria, the Christians had risen up in 872 and overthrown the Viking client king, a man named Ecgberht, replacing him with their own, Ricsige. However, Halfdan now intervened and made himself king, until he came to a sticky if improbable end in 877, when according to the Anglo-Saxon sources, he was heard prominently insulting St Cuthbert and then soon after, began to "rave and reek so badly that his whole army drove him from its midst". Another chronicle, the *Annals of Ulster*, say he was killed in 877 in a battle with the Irish, which admittedly sounds more plausible.

But Cuthbert continued to have immense power, indeed his career went from strength to strength, despite being dead. For one thing, even the pagans seemed to have developed a certain wariness about his cult; there was another story involving a Viking trying to break into Cuthbert's shrine at Chester-le-Street and the floor opening up and swallowing him straight to hell. Cuthbert's cult was now significant enough that it had become something of a revenue stream to Durham cathedral, and to the diocese generally.

According to the *Chronicle*, Cuthbert now appeared in a vision to Eadred, the abbot of Carlisle, telling him to go to the Danes and tell them that they should find a young man called Guthred, "son of Harthacanute, the slave of a certain widow", and "lead him before the whole multitude so that they may elect him king and at the ninth hour lead him with the whole army upon the hill which is called Oswigesdune and there place on his right arm a golden armlet, and thus they shall all constitute him king". Whatever the bizarre backstory behind this, this Guthred did become the Christian king of Northumbria from 883, although he insisted that the body of St Cuthbert be officially put in charge of the country, handing "over to the community all the lands between the Rivers Tyne and Wear" to the corpse, now ruler of the kingdom.

After the defeat of Guthrum some of the crazier Vikings had gone off to Francia, led by a warrior called Haesten, who as a young man had joined Ragnar on the voyage to attack Rome and ended up buying slaves from North Africa and bringing them to Ireland; in the name of religious equality his party had also sacked and burned down the mosque at Algeciras in Moorish Spain.

The Frankish king Louis III chased out the Norsemen at a pitched battle at Saucourt, close to the river Somme in 881, but the following year he died after falling off his horse while chasing a girl he had amorous designs on, a quintessentially French death if ever there was one. Now in 884 some Norsemen returned to England, hanging around East Anglia and making a nuisance of themselves; Alfred sent messages to Guthrum and his followers to help defend the country but heard nothing back from them. Then in 885 the Vikings assembled on the Thames estuary.

The Danes next landed in Kent and took Rochester castle, an important military position for anyone wanting to control the Thames; they were joined by other Vikings in Essex, and soon enough Guthrum got involved with his old Viking friends. But England was now better protected, thanks to Alfred, for under his burh system Wessex had 27,000 men available to defend it at any time. It also had a navy.

The Vikings were pre-eminent seamen, which was why they were such a menace everywhere from Ireland to Constantinople. To counter this Alfred built a fleet of ships and trained men to sail them, so that by 910 there were 100 boats in his fleet. Although Victorians saw him as a spiritual father of the Royal Navy this might be exaggerating it a little bit; he did however take a personal hand in designing large ships, using Greek and Roman technology which he had personally sought out in old books. His forces won numerous subsequent sea battles, although critics point out that Alfred may have been too influenced by great classical dreams, and his very large ships of sixty oars were actually quite ineffective against the smaller, more nimble Danish boats.

In 885, the West Saxon navy beat a force of Danish ships and took all the booty, but were attacked on their return to land, before Alfred and his elder son Edward reacted quickly and drove the invaders back east. The new Viking expedition culminated in yet another peace treaty with Guthrum, in which Alfred expanded Wessex to include a key prize.

Roman Londinium had been largely deserted since the downfall of the empire. The Middle Saxons had built their settlement a mile west, calling it Lundenwic, which came under the control of Mercia in the eighth century, although with Viking attacks more people may have begun moving inside the old Roman walls for protection.

Now Alfred re-founded the old city "splendidly", as Asser put it in his characteristic unbiased way, with the Roman walls rebuilt. The Saxon settlement of Lundenwic to the west came to become known as the "old city", or Aldwych—now London's theatre district—while across the river Alfred established a burh called the "Surrey defence work", or Southwark, which would become the city's seedy underbelly.

This appears to be an important moment when the concept of England came a step closer; Alfred was no longer just king of the West Saxons, for in 886, in the newly rebuilt city of Lundenburh, the *Chronicle* recalls that "all the English people that were not under subjection to the Danes submitted to him". Asser wrote: "All the Angles and Saxons ... turned willingly to King Alfred and submitted themselves to his lordship." He was, in the eyes of the people, *rex Anglorum*—king of the English. When Alfred made peace with Guthrum, he came with "the councillors of all the English race", according to documents, suggesting he was representing them all; charters from the late 880s now describe Alfred as "king of the Angles and of the Saxons". For the first time, after numerous *bretwalda* who had claimed supremacy, one man did rule what was left of the English nation.

To shore up his power in the Midlands, Alfred's daughter Ethelfleda had been married to Ethelred, an ealdorman in Mercia. Alfred fought alongside his son-in-law on several occasions, and gave him a sword worth 3,000 pennies, equivalent to 300 acres of land. With this marriage alliance, the dream of a united England came closer.

Meanwhile Guthrum seems to have become quite keen on Christianity, and encouraged conversion among his subjects; the Danes in East Anglia even started making commemorative coins of St Edmund, even though it was they who'd killed him only twenty years before. By the time that Guthrum died in 890, he was almost a reformed man.[68]

Yet the fighting never really ended. New Vikings turned up—there just seemed to be an endless supply of them—but Haesten was still the most threatening. His Viking army returned from Francia in 892, with as many as 250 pirate ships and after they landed in east Kent they were joined by another eighty vessels, having managed to recruit various random freebooters and criminals along the way.[69] The Viking armies of the 890s were even bigger than those of twenty years earlier, but the Saxons were ready.

Before the battle Haesten had sent his two sons for baptism as a statement of his good intent, planning to ignore it afterwards. Alfred and his son-in-law Ethelred stood as godfathers to the boys, perhaps hopeful that this would finally turn the old pirate to God, even though this policy consistently failed every time it was tried.

Despite Danish risings in Northumbria and East Anglia the Vikings were once again defeated and while Haesten was in the east his two sons were captured in Essex. The Viking might well have expected his children to be at best ransomed or even murdered, and many rulers of the time would have chosen the latter course, indeed seen anything else as weakness; Alfred returned them unharmed, and even sent them away with some presents. He was, after all, the boys' godfather, even though Haesten had absolutely no intention of honouring his baptismal promises. It was a supreme show of mercy.

What was left of the Danish force marched along the River Severn but an English army led by Ethelred was far too organised, and able to summon men from across the West. The last Danish holdout was at Buttington in Powys, where seventy skeletons were discovered in the nineteenth century.

There was now just Haesten's East Anglian army and in the autumn of 894 the old Viking left his ships to local Danes and marched northwest to Chester, then a ruined old Roman city, but by the spring they were running out of food. Many of the Vikings now gave up; for some reason one group went on to attack Anarawd ap Rhodri, King of Gwynedd, who had been their ally before. A second bunch of Vikings, led by someone called Sigeferth, fled across the Irish Sea where they attacked some other Vikings in Dublin. Haesten finally gave up in 897 and went to France. He had led a supremely adventurous life, travelling the world, experiencing an array of vastly different cultures and meeting lots of new people, and killing them.

And so Alfred finally had peace and a relatively easier life—for three years, before he died in October 899, short of his fiftieth birthday, having freed his personal servants and field labourers in his will. The *Chronicle* reports that "Here departed Alfred, son of Ethelwulf six nights before All Hallows Mass. He was King over all the English people [*Angel cyn*] except that part which was under the power of the Danes." The king's mission to save Wessex and England completed, he was buried in Winchester.

"No man should desire a soft life," Alfred once wrote. He certainly didn't get one.

CHAPTER 8

The first king of England

Within a generation Alfred's family had taken back all the lands under Danish rule; his son and daughter would extend their rule over all the land south of the Humber, and his grandson would become the first king of England. In doing so they established a dynasty whose descendants still rule the country today.

Alfred's marriage to Ealhswith of Mercia produced five surviving children; Ethelfleda and Edward, born between 874 and 877, were followed by Ethelgifu, Ethelweard, and Elfthryth. Of Alfred's wife we know very little—Asser didn't even bother mentioning her.

Elfthryth was married off to Baldwin, the son of Alfred's stepmother Judith, by her third husband "Baldwin of Iron Arm". Most of young Baldwin's time was spent fighting off Vikings, alas, but they were hard to escape at the time; their descendant Matilda would come to marry William the Bastard, Duke of Normandy, who is to feature prominently in later English history. Under the terms of Alfred's will his elder son Edward inherited the throne, and Ethelfleda was in effect in joint command of Mercia, while the youngest Elfrida only got three villages in Kent.[70]

Edward had been fighting Danes from a very young age and so was the natural choice, but Alfred's nephew Ethelwold technically had a better claim than his cousin. So after Edward was chosen as successor, Ethelwold went off to the Danelaw where he was proclaimed king in a cack-handed attempt to seize the crown from Alfred's son; it ended in failure and Ethelwold was killed in 903, along with a large number of Danes. The defeat of Ethelwold was perhaps the first case where the burhs system proved to work, by allowing a Viking army to be isolated and defeated.[71]

The new king became known to history as Edward the Elder[ii] and spent most of his life fighting the Danes. Edward was crowned at a location close to the borders of Mercia, Kent, and Wessex called Kings-Town upon Thames, where his son's coronation is still immortalised on a stone. Most of Edward's achievements were in fighting but he did also build an abbey in Winchester and in 903 he buried his mother there. His sister is perhaps even more important, although half-forgotten. Ethelfleda—or Ethelflæd—and her husband Ethelred had run Mercia together and after he died in 912 she ruled the kingdom, continuing Alfred's policy of building burhs, including Stafford, Warwick, and Runcorn; Wareham, one of the fortifications she constructed, was so effective it was still being used in the Second World War for anti-tank ditches.[72]

Ethelfleda went on to conquer the rest of Mercia from the Danes, aiding her brother as he gradually annexed all of England below the Humber. She became known as The Lady of the Mercians and a warrior queen of great standing, something that was quite exceptional for the period when career paths for women were somewhat limited.

Ethelfleda also seems to have had an unusually strategic mind. In 907 she had Chester refortified, giving her control of the Mersey and Dee, which provoked an invasion of Norwegian Vikings based in Ireland. But the Mercian queen outwitted them; feigning retreat, her forces fled to the city where they were pursued by the Vikings who followed them into the walls, where inside was a posse of concealed horsemen. Once these Vikings were inside, the gates closed and they were all killed, while the rest of the force besieged the city. And here the English won a famous victory, pouring boiling beer and then beehives on the besiegers, according to the *Chronicle*. Sadly, spoilsport historians tend to be

---

[ii] He was originally called Edward I but the naming system was restarted after 1066, largely by accident, because there were three Edwards in a row from 1272–1377 and people just got used to referring to them as Edward I, II, and III to differentiate them. And now it's too late to change back the system.

quite sceptical about this element of the story, which may have gained something in the retelling, killer bees being slightly implausible weapons for the time.

Three years later the Vikings again attacked English Mercia, only to be pushed back and defeated at Tettenhall by a combined Mercian and West Saxon force. By now Ethelred was dying, but following his death, Ethelfleda continued to build burhs along the border with Wales. She then set about capturing the area known as the Five Boroughs, what is today East Midlands, so splitting Norse-held territory in two and giving out the newly conquered land to her thegns.

In 910 a great Viking army attacked western Mercia but were slaughtered, with three Danish kings "hastening to the hall of the Infernal One" as the scribes put it. Pushing back, in 917 Ethelfleda took Derby, a former Viking stronghold, then Colchester. By Christmas all the Vikings of East Anglia had pledged that "they would do everything as he [Edward] commanded them to do".

When, the previous year, a Mercian abbot was killed in the Welsh kingdom of Brycheiniog, the Lady of Mercia summoned the local king, Tedwr, but he didn't bother replying, perhaps thinking a female ruler could be ignored. She turned up with an army and beat his men in battle; suitably cowed, Tedwr would later appear as a witness to her successor's charter.

When Ethelfleda died, on June 12, 918, she was referred to by the *Annals of Ulster* as "The most-famous Queen of the Saxons". Ethelfleda was buried in Gloucester but despite her pivotal role has been largely forgotten by history, at least until the twenty-first century. The Mercian nobles wanted her daughter Elfwynn as their monarch, but instead Edward had his sister's body removed to Gloucester and her daughter brought to the south, where she was eventually put in a convent.

Before the old king had died, Edward had a liaison with a woman called Edgina, who was either an aristocrat or a shepherdess he had spotted while out hunting, depending on how romantic and/or creepy you like your stories, and the woman became a "noble concubine of [Edward's] youth", according to one description. Soon a son was born.

The boy's name was Athelstan, and he came to be doted on by his grandfather before the old man's death. However, Edward dumped Edgina when he needed an alliance, and took a new wife, Elflaed, for dynastic reasons, with whom he had several children; Edgina was also packed off to a convent and their young son was sent to live with his aunt. Without a mother, and with his father now married to another woman, the young Athelstan was raised by his aunt in Mercia. Then, after Ethelfleda's death, Edward needed a new alliance to win over some Vikings, and so Elflaed was also sent off to the nunnery and replaced with Eadgifu, the daughter of Sigehelm, ealdorman of Kent. Edward wasn't going to win any awards for husband or father of the year.

Edward died in 924, and according to *The History of St Cuthbert*, written a century later by the monks at Durham, now home to a thriving shrine to St Cuthbert, he summoned his son Athelstan "and diligently instructed [him] to love St Cuthbert and honour him above all saints, revealing to him how he had mercifully succoured his father King Alfred in poverty and exile".

So Athelstan took the throne, despite Edward having had another thirteen surviving children, and his parents not being married. Athelstan was lucky in that his rival claimant, his half-brother Ethelweard, died within a few weeks. This was from natural causes; less natural was the mysterious fate of another half-brother Eadwine, who tried to seize the throne in 933 and who washed up on the coast a few days later having been exiled, although it's unlikely Athelstan actually had him murdered. After Eadwine's death, however, Athelstan felt so guilty he set up a monastery at Milton Abbas in Dorset.

It's probable that Edward had nominated Ethelweard to succeed him but the leading men of Mercia had got together and chosen Athelstan instead, a man they were more familiar with; we'll never know, because not only is history written by winners, but in this period the losers couldn't even read. Throughout his reign the new king remained an outsider in Wessex, and we know there were frosty relations with the New Minster at Winchester, guardians of his father's and half-brother's remains. But whatever the intricacies of politics between the two former kingdoms, the new king turned out to be a great king, the last of the *bretwaldas* and the first king of England.[73]

By now only the Viking kingdom of York lay outside Athelstan's control and when in 927 its king Sitric died, he immediately took the opportunity to annex the Viking kingdom. The local elders accepted his rule over all of the former Northumbrian kingdom, making July 12, 927, the date on which the unity of England was formally recognised.

In fact he didn't stop there, marching all the way to northern Scotland to battle King Constantine, after the Scots ruler had failed to acknowledge him as overlord. During his trip he also attacked the previously attacked Bamburgh castle in Northumbria because the local earl, Ealdred Ealdulfing, did not bow to his authority. From 927 to 934 there would be peace in the North, which for the standards of the time was an age.

Viking York had developed a strong and distinctive culture of its own, mixing Scandinavian, Saxon, and Irish influences; although it became an important trading centre and produced all sorts of coins of interest to specialists in that area, as well as bone-combs, perhaps the most curious thing found there is the "world's largest human coprolite", that is, fossilised faeces.

Despite promising never to deal with "idol worshippers", in 937 Constantine had gone into alliance with Olaf of Guthfrithson, Viking king of Dublin who claimed Northumbria, as well Owain of Strathclyde, the Welsh-speaking kingdom of western Scotland. They marched south, and the two armies met at the Battle of Brunanburh where Athelstan won a spectacular (but mostly forgotten) victory, leading an army of West Saxons, Mercians, East Anglians, and Northumbrians. It was perhaps the most important event in early English history, estimated to involve as many as 15,000 on each side, larger than that at Hastings in 1066, and was known at the time as "the great war"; it appears not just in the *Anglo-Saxon Chronicle* but in various Norse, Celtic, and Latin chronicles, and even in the Icelandic sagas.

An Anglo-Saxon poem about the battle states that at the end of the day five young kings lay dead: "Stretched lifeless by the sword, and with them seven of Olaf's earls and a countless host of seamen of Scots". The poem continues: "Never in this island before now, so far as the books of our ancient historians tells us, has an army been put to greater slaughter at the edge of the sword, since the time when the Angles and Saxons made their way hither from the east over the wide seas, invading Britain, when warriors eager for glory, proud forgers of battle, overcame the Britons and won for themselves a country."

Yet today so little is remembered of the great Battle of Brunanburh that there are forty possible locations for the conflict, among them Dumfriesshire, Northumberland, Cheshire, and Wiltshire. Somewhere in Cumbria or maybe Durham seems to be the most likely, although a golf club in Merseyside is still claimed as a location and at one point, there were plans for a Viking theme park based on the idea, so let's hope for their sakes they're right.

Where Athelstan did not use violence to conquer Vikings, he used sex. Sitric of York, who had gone by the rather grand title, "King of the

Fair Foreigners and the Dark Foreigners", had been married off to one of Athelstan's sisters before his death. Athelstan had nine half-sisters to marry off in total; when in 929 Henry the Fowler, king of Saxony, asked for a bride for his son Otto, the English king sent two of his sisters to Germany to let the king choose. How depressing the journey back must have been for the one not picked.

Athelstan in 926 had married his sister Ealdhild to Hugh the Great, king of the Franks, and the dowry included not just perfumes, horses, an onyx vase, jewels, and the swords of Constantine and Charlemagne, but the lance that pierced Christ and "a small piece of the holy and wonderful Cross enclosed in Crystal". Athelstan had become something of a player in international politics, giving aid to his godson Alain of Brittany in his fight against Vikings. Alain "of the twisted beard" was so tough he liked to hunt bears with a stick rather than a spear, hitting them over the head.

After his victory in York Athelstan now went by the title *rex Anglorum*, king of the English on his coins; for the first time in history, one man ruled England. Although the kings of Wessex had united the country, much of it had a very large Danish population, but when Athelstan took over the Danelaw he did not replace the Viking aristocracy; instead those listed as swearing to him were, their names suggest, the sons and grandsons of Danes who had settled in the ninth century. Athelstan did, however, encourage Saxon thegns to buy land in Viking territories to Anglicise them. Otherwise there doesn't seem to have been much hurry to assimilate them; Athelstan's nephew King Edgar decreed that the Danes should obey "such good laws as they best prefer".

The Vikings had changed the character of much of the country, the newcomers having built 1,400 towns and villages in the North and East with slightly harsh sounding names beginning with "Sc" or ending with "by", including Derby, Rugby, Grimsby, Scunthorpe, and Scarborough; today there are 850 places ending in "by" in England, over half of them in Yorkshire or Lincolnshire.

Yet within quite a short time the hostility between Saxons and Danes had softened; while the two groups would live in separate villages at first and presumably try their best to avoid each other, as time went by they began to communicate and, as is inevitable, to intermarry. It certainly helped that the two groups also had a similar language, but they were distinct enough to present communication difficulties, and as a result the neighbours were forced to drop the unnecessary verb endings and cases that make learning most Continental languages so difficult.

Old English was needlessly complicated before the Vikings arrived; it had three genders, while nouns could be spelt five different ways depending on the case, and adjectives had up to eleven forms. Even "the" was spelt nine ways depending on whether it was masculine, feminine, or neuter, single or plural. Afterwards many English words had as few as two different verb endings (I do, you do, he does, etc.), adjectives and nouns were standardised, and gender started to be phased out, a process finished under the Normans (today there are only extremely rare examples, like blond/blonde). That is why today German grammar looks utterly baffling, bordering on torture, to English speakers.

The Danes also added to the richness of our vocabulary, adding such words as *scream, take, clasp, anger, bang, berserk, clasp, cunning, gruesome, hit, rape, screech, scuffle, scream, slaughter, take,* and *skull*.

Of course, not all Norse-English words relate to violence, and without them we'd have no *wish* and *want, raise* and *rear, craft* and *skill, they, them,* and *their, big, baffled, build, both, glance, glimmer, gloat, kneel,* or *lift*. Yorkshire dialect in particular, which has given Standard English words such as *dollop, gawp,* and *nay,* is heavily Viking influenced. In the case of some verbs and nouns, both the Anglo-Saxon and Viking versions survived, eventually to develop subtle differences of meaning. *Craft*, an Anglo-Saxon word, and *skill*, which is Norse, originally had the same definition, and the same goes for *wish* and *want*, or *raise* and *rear*. So the Vikings made English a richer language, although whether the monks having the tops of their heads chopped off at the time would have appreciated this is a moot point.

Athelstan, like his grandfather, was an enlightened Christian monarch. Such was his reputation for learning that poets and scholars came to his court from all over western Christendom, and he was even asked to arbitrate on Continental disputes, helping to make Alan Twisted-Beard ruler of Brittany. Other leaders, such as Harold Fine Hair of Norway, sent their children to be fostered at his court, while Otto of Germany sent him books. He had a great interest in book-collecting and learning that was unusual at the time, and beyond his kingdom he had a reputation for amassing relics.[74] His court included Irish bishops, a Breton soldier, an Icelandic poet, and the greatest Continental scholar of his day, Israel the Grammarian.[75]

Athelstan's rule was aimed at "ensuring that the Christian ideals promoted and discussed at his court found expression in his legislative programme and that he governed his united realm as a truly Christian monarch", in the words of modern biographer Sarah Foot,[76] and when he was consecrated by the Archbishop of Canterbury, he became the first king to wear a crown (earlier kings had worn a helmet) as well as a ring, sword, and rod of office. Athelstan was also the first king to have a royal portrait, in which he appears with an imperial crown, his hair in ringlets entwined with threads of gold. He's probably the oldest ruler who a time traveller would look at and obviously recognise as a medieval king, as viewed in the popular imagination.

Athelstan was a great lawmaker who built on his grandfather's work. He abolished the death penalty for children under the age of fifteen for minor offences, which made him something like a barmy liberal for the tenth century, especially as children that age were still being executed on the cusp of the Victorian age. Athelstan was also the first lawmaker in England to provide poor relief, his code stating that "If a king's reeve failed to provide, from the rents of the royal demesne, for the poor in the manner prescribed he had to find 30 shillings to be distributed among the poor under the bishop's supervision."[77]

Not that we should get carried away, for the laws of Athelstan also "mention drowning or throwing from a cliff for free women, stoning for male slaves, burning for female slaves ... In the case of a male slave, sixty and twenty slaves shall go and stone him. And if any of them fails three times to hit him, he shall himself be scourged three times." This law states that for a female slave "who commits an act of theft anywhere except against her master or mistress, sixty and twenty female slaves shall go and bring three logs each and burn that one slave; and they shall pay as many pennies as male slaves would have to pay, or suffer scourging as has been stated above with references to male slaves."[78] Likewise, a law from the mid-tenth century describes one widow being sent to the king because she was found with dolls representing her victims and had driven nails into them—she was as a result drowned at London Bridge. So it wasn't quite a social democrat paradise.

Being a very religious man, the king reinvigorated the monastic movement, and was also addressed as *Rex pius Athelstan*, in a poem of that name which called him "Holy King Athelstan, renowned through the wide world"; while others called him "Emperor of the world of Britain", "king of the English", and *monarchus totius Britanniae*.

Having asserted his power over the whole country, Athelstan called national assemblies of bishops and lords for the first time, and also divided the Midlands into counties; he was also the first to define by law who got to mint coins across the country, an important aspect of royal authority. England was most certainly now a kingdom. An eleventh-century scribe from Exeter described Athelstan as a "king who ruled England alone which, before him, many kings had held among themselves". One poet, known only as Petrus and living at the time, wrote of him: "Whom he now rules with this Saxonia now made whole: King Athelstan lives glorious through his deeds." When he died in 939 the *Annals of Ulster* noted: "Athelstan king of the English died, the roof tree of the honour of the western world."

And yet not only is his great battle forgotten but the first king of England is largely unknown; his anniversary was barely noted in 1939, although in fairness we had other things to worry about, and if you asked the average person today what they thought of Athelstan, they'd probably guess it was some godforsaken place in central Asia.

This "roof tree of honour of the western world" was famous in the medieval period and was even mentioned in Shakespeare, and it was only from the sixteenth century that Athelstan became increasingly forgotten, as his grandfather became more famous. Perhaps it was because Alfred's narrative of having our backs against the wall is more attractive than Athelstan's story of cementing the legacy, or that Alfred had commissioned a biographer to record his great achievements, and that a series of attractive stories about him fired the imagination. There was, according to some sources, a biography of Athelstan written during his lifetime, but it was lost.

The only people who vaguely celebrate Alfred's grandson today are the Freemasons, who trace their origins to King Athelstan, but their interpretation of their own history can be imaginative, to put it kindly.

The Chronicle recorded how in 934, following the war, Constantine, king of Scotland as well as Owain, king of Strathclyde, three Welsh kings and their noblemen were now "rejoicing under the arms of [English] royal generosity". Rejoicing might not have been an entirely accurate description, in fairness.

Following the "Great Battle", as they called it, England would be one country, and it would inevitably dominate its smaller neighbours. It was probably in Athelstan's reign that *The Great Prophecy of Britain* came to be written, in which Welsh writers look forward to the destruction of the English, as foretold by Merlin. He said the Britons of Wales, Cornwall, and Strathclyde would join with Scots, Irish, and Vikings and drive the English out of Britain and "there will be heads split open without brains. Women will be widowed and horses riderless."

And yet the curious thing is that the myth of Arthur takes form during the reign of Athelstan, a king widely viewed as the exemplar of justice, a model of Christian kingship, as well as an unbeaten warrior who united Britain. Indeed, the most obvious influence on Arthur was this paragon of early medieval kinship, Athelstan—the most perfect Christian king, and unifier of England.

CHAPTER 9

Alfred's legacy

Alfred wanted the crown handed down on "the spear side and not to the spindle side", that is, for the throne to pass through the male line. Athelstan never had children; it may have been part of the agreement with his half-brothers that he had no heirs, and he was followed by his half-brother Edmund I, "the deed-doer" (939–946), who may have earned his proactive nickname after defeating the Scots king of Strathclyde, taking his two sons hostage, and having them blinded. Edmund spent most of his time fighting the remaining Vikings of York, but he had also made the historical appointment, in 941, of one "Oda" as Archbishop of Canterbury, the son of two Danish parents and the first Viking to ascend to the top job. His father was said to have served in the Great Heathen Army in 865 and here he was, head of the English Church. Truly the Obama moment of the mid-tenth century.

Edmund's potentially glorious reign was cut short when the king got into a fight with a gate crasher at a royal party, the brawl ending with king and intruder stabbing each other to death; this wasn't a time of great courtly etiquette and decorum. The unwanted guest, an exiled thief called Leofa, had threatened one of Edmund's servants, and under the customs of the day the king was expected to step into a fight involving his men. (An alternative, more boring explanation is that he was just assassinated.)

He was succeeded by his brother Eadred (946–955), who continued the conquest of Viking York, fighting its ruthless leader Eric Bloodaxe. Eric was a Viking so famously bloodthirsty that he murdered at least two of his own brothers—although he had about twenty to start with—before his untimely end. (Eric also went by the nickname "brother killer" although it should strictly speaking be *"brothers* killer".) Eventually he was killed by another Viking, and York was finally, fully pacified in the 950s, having been Viking for almost a century.

The Norsemen, it seems, were gone for good as a military threat. Eadred then had himself crowned with the rather grand title "King of the Anglo-Saxons, Northumbrians, Pagans and Britons", before dying of an unknown illness at the age of thirty-two (a pretty good age for the time, at least if you spent your time fighting Vikings). Anglo-Saxon monarchs loved to use quite overblown titles: Athelstan was "King of the Whole of Britain", Edmund was "King of the English and of other peoples, governor and director", while Edwig (955–959) was "King by the will of God, Emperor of the Anglo-Saxons and Northumbrians, governor of the pagans, commander of the British", and Edmund's other son Edgar styled himself "Autocrat of all Albion and its neighbouring realms".

All that we know of Eadred is that he had such disgusting table manners that his thegns would get drunk to distract themselves from the grotesque sight of watching him eat. The king would suck the juice out of his food, then chew it for a bit, before spitting it out, "a practice that often turned the stomachs of the thegns dining with him". This may have been the result of some mystery illness and by 955 he was dying.

This story is recounted in the Life of Bishop Dunstan, the great reforming figure of the time who came to power under King Edmund.[79] As a young man Dunstan had wanted to get married and was engaged to a woman called Elfheah, who presumably wasn't so keen on the idea and prayed for divine help. God sent blisters to break out all over his body, so Dunstan thought he had leprosy and agreed to become a monk.

St Dunstan, as he later became, was a very holy man but this also got on a lot of people's nerves, including Edmund who at one point had him banished until he was spooked by a near-death experience by Cheddar Gorge. Now Dunstan fell out with the new king, Edmund's sixteen-year-old tearaway son Edwig, whose proto-rock star antics were not appreciated by chroniclers. Edwig caused an outrage by failing to turn up to his own coronation in Kingston, and Bishop Dunstan was so angry that he marched to the king's nearby quarters, where he found the teenager in bed with a "strumpet" and the strumpet's mother. Dunstan's biographer says of Edwig and the women, he "took it in turns to subject them to his lustful attention".

The chroniclers noted that he was "disporting himself disgracefully between the two women, as if they were wallowing in some revolting pigsty". Absolutely disgusting.

The fact that the "strumpet" was his cousin probably didn't do his case much good. Edwig went on to do the decent thing by marrying the young woman, until the Church decreed that, as she was related, the marriage was illegal.[80] Dunstan, however, had to flee the country, with the king following him to his monastery in Flanders and plundering it. Luckily for the bishop the excitable young monarch died mysteriously a couple of years later, by which time he had already made himself so unpopular that the kingdom was briefly split, with the North in rebellion.

So the crown passed to his brother Edgar, and it is with Edgar that the kingdom of England was finally established; indeed when subsequent kings wanted to affirm their right to rule they would generally cite Edgar's reign as being the time when everything worked. By this time the country was divided into shires and hundreds, or *wapentake* as they were called in the Danelaw, the divisions that made it possible to have a fully functional legal system; these shires, or *counties* as they came to be known after the Norman conquest, became the basic subdivision of government in the English-speaking world.

Edgar was so powerful that he had three coronation ceremonies, first in Kingston and then towards the end of his reign in Bath and Chester, just to show who was boss; after that he had seven Scots and Welsh kings row him on the River Dee, illustrating his dominance. At his coronation in Bath, most likely held there because of the association with Rome, a bishop placed the crown on the king's head, creating a ceremonial tradition so enduring that it was in many ways the same as that of his descendant Charles III in 2023 (give or a take a few television cameras). The country would be ruled as one—Alfred's family had finally achieved the unity of England.

Yet there would be trouble ahead, in the form of renewed Viking and Norman conquests, and Alfred's direct male line died out in 1126 with Edgar the Atheling, who as a boy in 1066 was unable to challenge the invasion of William the Conqueror. Alfred's descendants, though, have spread around the globe; but more important is his political legacy.

While Athelstan's star faded in the medieval period, Alfred's rose, and so by the fifteenth century the feeble-minded Henry VI was trying to have him made a saint. This didn't happen, but Alfred is today the only English king to be styled "the Great", and it was a word attached to him from quite an early stage. Even in the twelfth century the gossipy chronicler Matthew Paris is the first person to call him "the Great", and says it's a common phrasing.

However, much of what is recorded of him only became known in Tudor times, partly by accident. Henry VIII's break from Rome was to have a huge influence on our understanding of history, chiefly because so many of England's records were stored in monasteries.[81]

Before the development of universities, these had been the main intellectual centres in Christendom, indeed from where universities would grow, and where most chronicles were written or stored. Now, along with relics, huge amounts of them would be lost, destroyed, sold ... or preserved.

It was lucky that Matthew Parker, a sixteenth-century Archbishop of Canterbury with a keen interest in history, had a particularly keen interest in Alfred. It was Parker who published Asser's *Life of Alfred* in 1574, having found the manuscript after the dissolution of the monasteries, a book that found itself in the Ashburnham collection amassed by Sir Robert Cotton in the late sixteenth and early seventeenth centuries. Sadly, however, while copies were made in the meantime, the original *Life* was burned in a famous fire at Ashburnham House in Westminster on October 23, 1731. Boys from nearby Westminster School had gone into the blaze alongside the owner and his son to rescue manuscripts, but much was lost, among them the only surviving manuscript of the *Life of Alfred*, as well as that of *Beowulf*. In fact the majority of recorded Anglo-Saxon history had gone up in smoke in minutes.

A copy of *Beowulf* had also been made, although the poem only became widely known in the nineteenth century. The fire also destroyed the oldest copy of the Burghal Hidage, a unique document listing towns of Saxon England and provisions for defence made during the reign of Edward the Elder. An eighth-century illuminated gospel book from Northumbria was also lost.

So it is lucky that Parker had had *The Life of Alfred* printed, even if he had made alterations in his copy that to historians are infuriating because they cannot be sure if they are authentic. He probably added the story about the cakes, for instance, although this had come from a different Anglo-Saxon source.

We also know that Archbishop Parker was a bit confused, or possibly just lying; he claimed Alfred had founded his old university, Oxford, which was clearly untrue, and he was probably trying to make his alma mater sound grander than Cambridge. Oxford university dates from the twelfth century, Cambridge a bit later, and in Alfred's time the village of Oxford would have been no more than a few huts. Having said that, the myth that he founded the university in 886 dated back to the thirteenth century and was even officially recognised by the authorities, so he may have been genuinely mistaken. People in the past often assumed things were a lot older than they actually were.

Alfred's popularity continued to rise over time. Sir John Spelman's version of the *Life* was published in 1642–1643, apparently for the edification of King Charles I, which obviously didn't work, as he ended up being beheaded by his own people.

The oldest memorial to Alfred is a pub, dating from 1763, when John and Elizabeth Stevens of Wantage opened their new inn in Alfred's home town, called "Alfred's Head".

Alfred was among sixteen people included in the Temple of British Worthies, an eighteenth century feature of Stowe House, Buckinghamshire, one of the great country homes of the period, and he was one of only three monarchs to make the cut. His popularity reached a peak in the eighteenth and nineteenth centuries; when in 1740 the royal court celebrated the accession of Alfred's German successor George I, Thomas Arne wrote an opera, *Alfred*, about the king who had been father to the nation (among its seven songs was *Rule Britannia*).

Alfred became the epitome of heroic kingship, justice, and liberty, praised in poems by Shelley and Wordsworth; it was partly helped by the fact that we know so little of him, but also that the monarchs of the age seemed the exact opposite. George I, the first of a series of witless, boorish morons to compose the House of Hanover, had been cuckolded by a Swede, who he then had murdered, and had his wife locked in a dungeon for thirty-odd years until her death; the exact opposite of Alfred, in other words. By William Wordsworth's time the country was ruled by George III, who was insane, and who was followed by the debauched, grossly obese playboy, the former Prince Regent, now George IV. The upright Victorian period, a reaction to this decadent aristocratic lifestyle, therefore idealised Alfred, who was referred to as "England's Darling" in one poem.

Schoolchildren were now taught the story of the king and the cakes as part of national folklore, the king epitomising everything that was good in the English character. The Victorians especially loved Alfred, considering him to have all the qualities that made a great Englishman: courage, fortitude, learning, sexual neurosis. Around 10,000 people turned up to a millennial celebration of Alfred's birth in 1849 in Wantage organised by a sort of Victorian moralist called Martin Tupper whose odes to "King of a race that reigns and rejoices in every place" would probably not be taught in schools today.[82]

Fans also marked the millennial anniversary of his death with a ceremony in Winchester in which universities from Britain, America, and the other English-speaking countries put up a statue, raised at the cost of £5,000. Unfortunately, they got the actual year wrong, as this was done in 1901, when he actually died in 899. There was also an exhibition at the British Museum, and among the items on display were passages from the *Anglo-Saxon Chronicle*, a copy of Asser's *Life*, as well as some of the books Alfred translated and illuminated gospels from the era. There were also some jewels, including two gold rings, one belonging to Ethelwulf, which had been found in Wiltshire in 1780, and picked up by a labourer who sold it for thirty-four shillings. The other had been commissioned by Alfred's sister, Ethelswith, Queen of Mercia, and bears the title *Eathelswitha Regna*; it was discovered in Yorkshire in the 1870s.

But in the wider scheme of things these trinkets are not important; his lasting legacy is the institutions around us, both in England and those countries that derive their political systems from the Anglo-Saxons. Alfred, having rescued the country from conquest, helped to establish one of the oldest and longest-lasting of nation states, whose inhabitants have been lucky to enjoy stable institutions and the rule of law for most of the time since. He also brought the country's culture back in touch with Europe, spreading literacy and knowledge of the Latin world—for all this it's right to call him the Great.

The 1901 parade also passed into Winchester Cathedral, last resting place of numerous Saxon kings, among them Alfred's father and grandfather, Ethelwulf and Egbert; yet the whereabouts of the bones of England's founder remain a mystery. Edward the Elder had his parents' bodies reinterred at the Minster in Winchester, but in the twelfth century Alfred's Norman descendant Henry I had them reburied in Hyde Abbey. Unfortunately, it was destroyed in the Reformation and his remains were lost; the site then became a prison and during rebuilding work all the bones in the former grounds of the abbey were scattered.

It seems wrong that the man who founded the nation is buried under an old prison in Hampshire rather than under a 300 ft monolith in the centre of the capital. However, after the discovery of Richard III's body under a car park in Leicester in 2012 there was renewed hope in finding Alfred; Richard's corpse had been lost after the abbey where it was buried was ransacked by religious fanatics (as it happened, the body of Henry I also turned up in 2014 under yet another car park, his resting place of Reading Abbey having also been destroyed in the Reformation).

By this stage archaeologists from the University of Winchester had in fact already been analysing six skeletons found at St Bartholomew's church, built on the site of Hyde Abbey. They looked at some bones discovered in the 1990s and concluded that a hipbone dated to the time of Alfred and probably belonged to a member of his family, most likely Alfred, Edward, or his brother Ethelweard, although unlike in Richard III's case there were no direct male or female descendants to make the match—so perhaps we'll never know.

The search continues, but perhaps it doesn't matter. His real legacy is England, its customs and freedom, a people descended from both Saxons and Vikings under the rule of law. Cuthbert was right: all Albion was given to him and his sons.

BIBLIOGRAPHY

This book is an introduction to the subject, as the title probably suggests, and far more can be discovered in detail in the following books:

Ackroyd, Peter *Foundation*
Ackroyd, Peter *London*
Adams, Max *The King in the North*
Adams, Max *Alfred's Britain*
Albert, Edoardo and Tucker, Katie *In Search of Alfred the Great*
Ashley, Mike *British Kings and Queens*
Brooke, Christopher *The Saxon and Norman Kings*
Brownworth, Lars *Sea Wolves: A History of the Vikings*
Bryson, Bill *Mother Tongue*
Campbell, James (ed.) *The Anglo-Saxons*
Clements, Jonathan *Vikings*
Crossley-Holland, Kevin *The Anglo-Saxon World*
Foot, Sarah *Athelstan: The First King of England*
Fraser, Antonia *The Lives of the Kings and Queens of England*
Frere, Sheppard *Britannia: A History of Roman Britain*
Higham, Nicholas J., and Ryan, Martin J. *The Anglo-Saxon World*
Hindley, Geoffrey *The Anglo-Saxons: A Brief History*
Holland, Tom *Athelstan: The Making of England*

Jackson, Dan *The Northumbrians*
Jarman, Cat *River Kings*
Lacey, Robert *Great Tales from English History (Part One)*
Lees, Beatrice Adelaide *Alfred the Great: The Truth Teller, the Maker of England*
Manco, Jean *The Origins of the Anglo-Saxons*
McKilliam, A. E. *The Story of Alfred the Great*
Morris, Mark *The Anglo-Saxons*
Oliver, Neil *The Vikings: A History*
Ormod, W. M. *The Kings and Queens of England*
Palmer, Alan *Kings and Queens of England*
Parker, Philip *The Northmen's Fury*
Pollard, Justin *Alfred the Great*
Price, Neil *Children of Ash and Elm*
Price, Neil *The Viking Way*
Ramirez, Janina *The Private Lives of the Saints*
Schama, Simon *A History of Britain Part One*
Shippey, Tom *The Road to Middle Earth*
Speck, W. A. *A Concise History of Britain*
Stenton, Sir Frank *Anglo-Saxon England*
Stone, Norman (ed.) *The Makers of English History*
Strong, Roy *The Story of Britain*
Tombs, Robert *The English and Their History*
White, R. J. *A Short History of England*

ENDNOTES

1. Some question whether this was really the first Viking attack on England, but since this is literally the Dark Ages there is going to be a lot of uncertainty over a lot of things.
2. Canute (1016–1035) is known as the Great in his native Denmark. He will feature a great deal in Part Two of this series.
3. From Robert Tombs, *The English and Their History*. Marcus Aurelius and Alfonso X of Castile are the rulers in question.
4. Again, this might not have happened. Some think this letter doesn't refer to Britain but to a town in southern Italy.
5. Also called *Apocalypse*, it describes a series of catastrophic events featuring a number of alarming figures such as "the Whore of Babylon" and "the Beast". As far back as the fourth century Church leaders considered taking it out, as it was so prone to be misinterpreted, while nineteenth-century humanist writer Robert Ingersoll described it as "the insanest of all books".
6. The etymology of Andalusia is disputed.
7. Tribes in the Low Countries tried to get around the problem by building their homes on artificial mounds, but eventually even they fled.
8. Ackroyd, Peter *Foundations*.
9. Ackroyd Peter *Foundations*.

112   ENDNOTES

10. Most historians don't think that's how Portsmouth got its name. It's more likely to be from the Portus harbour.
11. The exact date of their arrival is disputed. They may have arrived as early as 1000 BC.
12. Stephen Oppenheimer suggested the Anglo-Saxon input could be as low as 5.5 per cent, although that is probably too low.
13. Although the people who live there now have lots of DNA from the ancient Britons as since then people have all moved around the country.
14. Some people think Ambrosius is a different person altogether, though no one can really know.
15. Wood.
16. https://twitter.com/NatTrustArch/status/1392255553678741513.
17. http://ajsefton.com/#!anglo-saxon-calendar/cldp.
18. An interesting thread on the divisions here. https://twitter.com/rfhirst/status/1626380092128792579.
19. https://twitter.com/katemond/status/661859261887197184.
20. Tombs, Robert *The English and Their History*.
21. The actual sources confirming the Saxons did worship the Norse pantheon are not overwhelming, but the likelihood is that they did.
22. We think. We can't be entirely sure of what they believed.
23. https://en.wikipedia.org/wiki/List_of_oldest_schools.
24. Wood, Michael *In Search of the Dark Ages*.
25. It most recently featured as the setting for the final scene of *The Force Awakens*.
26. Ramirez, Janina *The Private Lives of the Saints*. It wasn't so much a kingdom as a *Túath*, which was more like an area ruled by a clan.
27. Hindley.
28. 130 calf skins would be needed to make them.
29. In North Korea Kim Il Sung, who died in 1994, is Eternal President, Eternal General Secretary of the Workers' Party of Korea and Eternal Chairman of the National Defence Commission.
30. Jackson, Dan *The Northumbrians*.
31. Higham and Ryan.
32. Tombs, Robert *The English and Their History*.
33. Although Greek scholar Procopius (500–554), considered the last "ancient" historian, had spoken of the people of the island being called the "Angiloi".
34. This is not unique. John the Baptist, if the relics are all genuine, had no fewer than three heads. No wonder the authorities were so scared of him.
35. This is by no means the oldest customer complaint in history; in the British Museum is a clay tablet from Babylonia dating to around 1750 BC,

written from a "Nanni" to someone called Ea-Nasir complaining about the copper ore he had bought. Whether Nanni ever got his copper ore we shall never know.
36. Woods, Michael *In Search of the Dark Ages*.
37. For centuries the Anglo-Saxons called the Germans "the Saxons overseas", after which they started referring to continental Germans as Dutch, from Deutsch. When the Netherlands split from Germany in the late Middle Ages this name stuck with England's closer neighbour, while the English started calling their more distant neighbours by the Latin term German. As fans of American Civil War films will know, until relatively late Germans in the United States were called "Dutchmen".
38. Or comes from "Vik", the name of a well-known fjord.
39. It was in fact the theatre director for Wagner's *Twilight of the Gods* who thought they'd look better this way.
40. Parker.
41. According to Clements.
42. Parker.
43. Clements, Jonathan.
44. Parker, Philip.
45. According to Saxo Gramaticus. From Lars Brownworth.
46. Again, and pedant alert, this may be disputed. Since many Vikings had visited Constantinople, they may have had a pretty good idea of what a big city looked like.
47. Parker.
48. Clement.
49. This is a scene borrowed by the TV series *Vikings*, although it is one of Ella's underlings who gets thrown in.
50. Ragnar is, of course, the main character in the television series *Vikings*, which also features other semi-legendary figures such as Bjorn, and Rollo, first ruler of Normandy, as well as historical figures like Egbert and Ethelwulf of Wessex.
51. The death of Aelle by a blood eagle is mentioned in an eleventh-century skaldic poem. As with so many stories of the time, its authenticity is dubious.
52. Bury means "town".
53. McKilliam.
54. King Ine's law code states that "From every group of ten hides under his rile, Ine expected an annual render of ten vats of honey, 300 loaves of bread, twelve "ambers" of Welsh ale, thirty of clear ale, two full-grown

cows or ten goats, ten geese, ten hens, ten cheeses, an amber of butter, five salmon, twenty pounds of fodder and a hundred eels."
55. An area so called because it takes its name from Berroc Wood where box trees grow.
56. And that historian is classicist and future mayor of London, prime minister of the UK and father of countless children, Boris Johnson.
57. Which was reported by Predentius of Troyes in his *Frankish Annals of Bertin*.
58. Philip Parker.
59. In the words of Tom Holland, author of *Athelstan*.
60. Albert, Edoardo.
61. There is some confusion about whether these might actually be the same person.
62. The Indian story is, admittedly, disputed. It is possible, however.
63. Parker.
64. Lees, Beatrice.
65. Campbell.
66. https://academia.edu/22980855/A_History_of_Beer_and_Brewing.
67. McKilliam.
68. Fans of 1960s British cinema might recall Michael York playing him in the 1969 film *Alfred the Great* during that period when there was a craze for Viking films.
69. McKilliam.
70. Lewisham, Woolwich, and Greenwich are now all areas in south-east London.
71. https://sagasfromthesea.blog/2023/03/27/aethelflaed-lady-of-mercia/.
72. Woods, Michael.
73. The claim to being a Bretwalda is sort of disputed but, since Athelstan became actual king of England, it hardly matters.
74. Stanton, Frank *Anglo-Saxon England*.
75. Wood, Michael.
76. Foot, Sarah.
77. Hostettler, John *A History of Criminal Justice in England*.
78. John Hamilton Baker (ed.) *The Oxford History of the Laws of England*.
79. Morris, Marc.
80. This story may be a slight embellishment, but what is known is that Dunstan and the king's bride and mother-in-law seem to have been at odds.
81. The Lindisfarne Gospels remained at Durham Cathedral until Henry VIII's goons stole them in the sixteenth century and brought them to London, and today the book rests at the British Library next to King's Cross station.
82. https://historytoday.com/archive/alfred-great-most-perfect-man-history.

INDEX

Adam of Bremen, 49
Alfred Jewel, 84
Alfred the Great, viii–ix, 66, 70, 77, 89
   Alfred Jewel, 84
   Anglo-Saxon Chronicle, 79–80
   ascent to Wessex throne, 71
   Asser, 77–78
   Battle of Countisbury Hill, 74
   Battle of Edington, 75
   benevolence and encounters with travelers, 81–82
   burnt bread story, 73–74
   Christianity, 19
   descent, 2
   "Doom book", 82
   early impressions of Rome, 67
   idealizing, 105–106
   John the Old Saxon, 79
   legacy, 101–107
   Life of Alfred, 77, 104–105
   lost resting place, 106–107
   maritime endeavors, 87
   marriage and children, 91
   national English legal system, 82–83
   pursuit of Roman glory, 81
   rebuilding London and uniting English nation, 87–88
   reforms, 83–84, 85
   restoring learning and literacy in England, 78
   rise of, 69–70
   siege of Chippenham and flight to Athelney, 73
   and the cakes, 73–74
   translations, 78–79
   Treaty of Edington, 76
   Viking challenge, 71
Angeln, 5
Anglo-Saxon(s), 1
   agriculture, 18
   arrival in Britain, 7, 12
   arrival in Britannia, 2
   art, 17–18
   British resistance to invasion, 14
   Cerdic, 11

Christianization of Kent, 22–23
class structure, 18
conversion of, 21–22
cultural practices, 18
culture and impact on Britain, 8
Dark Ages, 17
early Anglo-Saxon art, 17–18
early impact of Christianity, 21–24
Elle, 11
and English political system, 13
intra-kingdom struggles in
    Anglo-Saxon England, 29
invasion, 11
migration to Britain, 12
missionaries and Christianization
    of Germany, 43
origins of, 12
preservation and loss of history, 104
religion, 20
from Roman decline to
    Anglo-Saxon England, 1–9
settlement and abandoned
    Roman cities, 8
social hierarchy, 19
"Spong Man", 17
titles of monarchs of, 102
Vikings and, 54
Anglo-Saxon Chronicle, The, 2, 11, 17,
    79–80
Anglo-Saxon kings, 37–42. *See also*
    Alfred the Great
    Athelstan, ix, 93–100
    Cerdic, 2, 11, 63
    Charlemagne, 42
    Eadfrith, 31, 40
    Ecgfrith, 33, 44
    Edwin of Northumbria, 27–28
    Ethelbald, 41
    Ethelbert, 22–23
    Ethelfleda of Mercia, 92–93
    Ethelwulf of Wessex, 65–66
    Ine, 63, 113
    Offa, 41, 42–43, 44
    Osred of Northumbria, 40
    Oswald, 37
    Oswiu of Northumbria, 37–38
    Penda of Mercia, 40–41

Annals of Wales, 15
Anthony the Great, St., 30
Archbishop Parker. *See* Parker, Matthew
Armes Prydein Fawr (*The Prophecy
    of Britain*), 9
Arthurian legends, 14–16, 100
"assembly of drinkers, an", 83
Asser, 2, 77–78
Athelstan, ix, 93–94
    Battle of Brunanburh, 95
    conquests, 95
    diplomatic alliances, 95–96
    forgotten legacy of, 99–100
    interest in learning, 97
    laws of, 98
    from outsider to first King
        of England, 94–95
    Saxon and Danish coexistence and
        cultural transformation, 96
Augustine, St., 21–24

Bamburgh castle, 29
barbarians. *See also* Vikings
    of Britain, 22
    Franks, 42
    German communities and
        misadventures in Roman
        Britain, 5
    Huns, 3–4
    invasions of Roman empire, 3–4
    rise of barbarian mercenaries, 5
    Vandals, 3
Battle of Brunanburh, 95
Battle of Countisbury Hill, 74
Battle of Edington, 75
Bede. *See* Venerable Bede
Beowulf, 39–40, 104
blood eagle, 60
Boar's Head carol, 34
Boethius, 79
Boniface, St, 43
Bremen, Adam of, 49
Breton language, 9
Britain
    Anglo-Saxon culture and impact
        on, 8
    Anglo-Saxon migration to, 12

arrival of Anglo-Saxons in, 7
arrival of Germanic tribes in, 7
barbarians of, 22
British resistance to invasion, 14
Brittany, 9
Christianization of, 22–23
establishment of schools, 23
fall of Rome and dawn of dark
   ages in, 9
genetic tapestry of, 13–14
"Great Britain", 9
in shadow of volcanic eruptions
   and conquest, 17
written English law, 23–24
Britannia
   arrival of Angles and Saxons
      in, 2
   Gildas and prophecies of
      Britannia's doom, 2–3
   invasion and transformation
      of, 1–9
   post-Roman Britain, 5–6
Britons, 2, 7
   Breton language, 9
   Brittonic, 12
   Jutes' betrayal, 7
   language shifts, 12
   post-Roman Britain, 5–6
   Treachery of the Long Knives, 7
Brittany, 9
Brittonic, 12
burh system, 85, 87

Caedmon's Hymn, 39
Camelot myth, 16
Canute, 111
Cerdic, King, 2, 11, 63
Chad, St, 33, 65
Charlemagne, King, 42, 56
Cheddar Man, 13
Christianity, 19
   Christian missionaries, 23
   Christianization of Germany, 43
   Christianization of Kent, 22–23
   early impact of, 21
   Easter controversy and religious
      division in, 38
   heathens as agents of God's
      anger, 56
   Northumbria and, 26
Codex Amiatinus, 31
Codex Aureus, 58–59
Consolation of Philosophy, The, 79
cultural misunderstandings, vii
Cuthbert, St, 86
   Gospel, 31–32
Cymraeg, 9
cyrelif, 18

Danes, 19
Danish attacks, 85–89
Dark Ages, 17
   monasteries in Northumbria, 35
"Doom book", 82
Dunstan, St, 102

Eadbald, King, 24
Eadburh of Mercia, 64
Eadfrith, King, 31, 40
Eadred, King, 102
*Ecclesiastical History of the English
   Nation, The*, 35
Ecgfrith, King, 33, 44
Edgar the Atheling, 103
Edmund I, 101
Edmund, St, 60–61
Edward the Elder, 92, 93–94
Edwig, King, 102–103
Edwin of Northumbria, 27–28
Elle, Saxon warlord, 11
"Englalond", ix, 9
English
   ancestry, 13–14
   law, 23–24, 82–83
   Mercia, 92–93
   Norse-English words, 97
   Old English, 18, 97
   political system, 13
   Vikings influence on evolution
      of, 97
Eric Bloodaxe, 102
Ethelbald, King, 41
Ethelbert, King, 22–23
Ethelfleda of Mercia (Ethelflæd), 92–93

Ethelfrith the Ferocious, 24
Ethelwulf of Wessex, 65–66
    conspiracy against, 68–69
    legacy, 69
    vision and journey to Rome, 68
Europe, migration and invasions, 3

first king of England. *See* Athelstan
Franks, 11, 42
Freya, 51

Garman. *See* Anglo-Saxon(s)
German communities, 5
Gildas, 1
    about arrival of Anglo-Saxons
        in Britain, 7
    and prophecies of Britannia's
        doom, 2–3
Gododdin, 14
"Great Britain", 9

Haesten, 86, 88
Heliand, 43–44
Hen Ogledd, 6
Heptarchy, 22
human sacrifice and Norse
    religion, 49
Huns, 3–4

Ine, King, 63
    law code, 113
Irish monks, 30–31

John Dee, 25
John the Old Saxon, 79
Jutes, 6–7

last kingdom. *See* Wessex
Laws of Ethelbert, 23
legal system
    Athelstan, 98
    English law, 23–24
    Ine, 113
    Laws of Ethelbert, 23
    national English, 82–83
    Wihtred's laws, 24

"Lesser Britain". *See* Brittany
Life of Alfred, 104–105
Lindisfarne Gospels, 31, 114
Lindisfarne massacre, vii

Mercia, 41
    confusion in, 64–65
    Eadburh of Mercia, 64
    Ethelfleda of Mercia, 92–93
    Penda of Mercia, 27, 40–41
monasticism, 30
    Battle of the Book, 31
    Dark Ages monasteries
        in Northumbria, 35
    growth of, 39
    Irish monks, 30–31
    St. Anthony the Great, 30
    Whitby Abbey, 38, 39

naval innovation, 87
Nennius, 14, 15
Norse-English words, 97
Norse gods, 20
Norse religion
    afterlife in, 51
    Freya, 51
    human sacrifice and, 49
    Odin, 49–51
    origin story, 52
    Ragnarök, 52
    Valhalla, 50
Northumbrian golden age, 25
    Bamburgh castle, 29
    Battle of the Book, 31
    Codex Amiatinus, 31
    Eadfrith, 31, 40
    Edwin of Northumbria, 27–28
    formation and early history
        of Northumbria, 26
    holy mens, 31–33
    John Dee, 25
    kings, 40
    Lindisfarne gospels, 31
    monasticism, 30–31, 35
    from Paganism to
        Christianity, 34

rise of Oswald, 30
St Cuthbert Gospel, 31–32
Sutton Hoo's burial mound, 25–26
Venerable Bede, 35–36
warfare and kingship, 26–27

Odin, 49–51
Offa, King, 41
    Ecgfrith, 44
    influence of Francia and Roman imperialism, 43
    legacy, 44–45
    links to Francia, 42–43
Old English, 18, 97
Osred of Northumbria, 40
Oswald, King, 30, 37
Oswiu of Northumbria, 37–38

Parker, Matthew, 104, 105
Paulinus of York, 27
Penda of Mercia, 27, 40–41
Picts, 4
political system, English, 13
Pope Gregory I, 20–22, 34
Portsmouth, 112
post-Roman Britain, 5–6. *See also* Britain; Britannia; Britons; Roman empire
    language shifts and influences in, 12
Procopius, 112

Ragnar Lothbrok, 59, 113
Raven Floki, 47
Redwald of East Anglia, 26
Repton Warrior, 72
rex Anglorum. *See* Athelstan
Rex pius Athelstan. *See* Athelstan
"Roman climatic optimum", 4
Roman empire
    abandoned cities, 8
    barbarian invasions of, 3–4
    collapse of, 4
    decline and Christian resurgence, 20–21

    decline to Anglo-Saxon England, 1–9
    early impressions of, 67
    fall of Roman security, 4–5
    German communities and misadventures in Roman Britain, 5
    invasions of, 3–4
    post-Roman Britain, 5–6
    pursuit of Roman glory, 81
    "Roman climatic optimum", 4
    western empire, 4
Romano-British, 7
Rome
    Alfred's early impression of, 67
    Ethelwulf of Wessex to, 68
    fall of Rome and dawn of dark ages in Britain, 9
Ruin and Conquest of Britain, The, 1

Saesneg, 9. *See* Anglo-Saxon(s)
Saxons, 8, 11
    and Danish coexistence, 96
    invasions, 2
    mercenaries, 5
    method of architecture, 8
    scramaseax, 5
    spread and adaptation in western Europe, 11–12
"Saxon shore-forts", 3
"Saxony Overseas", 43
Scandinavia, 48
    fables and legends, 51–52
    Old Uppsala, 48–49
    origins and early history of, 48–49
    society, 53–54
scramaseax, 5
Sidonius Apollinaris, 8
Snorri's Edda, 53
"Spong Man", 17
St Peter's at Bradwell-on-the-Sea, 37
Sutton Hoo's burial mound, 25–26

Theodore of Canterbury, 32, 34
Treachery of the Long Knives, 7
Treaty of Edington, 76

Ubba, 74

Valhalla, 20
Vandals, 3
Venerable Bede, 35–36
Vikings, vii, 47
   and Anglo-Saxons, 54
   arrival in England, vii–viii
   Eric Bloodaxe, 102
   extortion and ransom, 58–59
   feasts and festivities, 51
   Haesten, 86, 88
   human sacrifice and Norse
      religion, 49
   incursions in England, 57–59
   influence on evolution of English
      language, 97
   invasion, vii–viii, 2, 55
   legacy of, 47–48
   myth of Viking warriors, 48
   Norse society, 53–54
   origins and early history
      of Scandinavia, 48–49
   origin story, 52
   Ragnar Lothbrok, 59
   raid, 57–58
   Raven Floki, 47
   religious conversion, 19
   Repton Warrior, 72
   settlements in Anglo-Saxon
      kingdoms, 72
   sex ratio, 56–57
   Snorri's Edda, 53
   St Edmund martyrdom, 60–61
   tactics, 60
   Ubba, 74
   voyages, 54

Viking York, 94, 95
Visigoths, 3
Vortigen, 6
   and arrival of Jutes, 6
   historical skepticism, 6
   Jutes' betrayal of, 7

warrior ethic, 17–19
Welsh, 9
Wessex, 63
   Alfred the Great, 66, 69–70, 70–76
   Beorhtric, 64
   burh system, 85, 87
   dynastic confusion in Mercia and
      rise of, 64–65
   Eadburh of Mercia, 64
   Ethelwulf of Wessex, 65–66,
      68–69
   Ine, 63
   inevitable Danish attacks, 85–89
   influence of St. Cuthbert, 86
   infrastructure development, 85
   kings of, 63–64
   naval innovation and Viking
      encounters, 87
   Norse invasions, 86–87
   Repton warrior, 72
   resistance to foreign rule, 85–86
   Viking settlements, 72
Whitby Abbey, 38, 39
Wihtred's laws, 24
Wilfred, St, 33–34, 38
Woden. *See* Odin
Wotan. *See* Odin
Wyrtgeorn. *See* Vortigen

"Ynglings, the", 48

Milton Keynes UK
Ingram Content Group UK Ltd.
UKHW021810241123
433186UK00011B/422